Public Relations : Strategies and Concepts

PUBLIC RELATIONS
STRATEGIES AND CONCEPTS

Naval Prabhakar
Narendra Basu

Commonwealth

Public Relations : Strategies and Concepts

Edition : 2022

ISBN 81-311-0029-4

Published by :
COMMONWEALTH PUBLISHERS PVT. LTD.
4831/24, Prahlad Street,
Ansari Road, Darya Ganj,
New Delhi - 110002
Ph. : 23275511, 23257835
e-mail : commonwealthbooks@gmail.com

Laser Typesetting by :
Rishu Computers
Delhi

Printed at :
Roshan Offset Printers
Delhi

Preface

Public relations is the art of creating mutual understanding between an organisation and its various publics including group or groups of people whose opinion has a direct bearing on the functioning of an organisation. It is an effective way to achieve smooth relationships, safeguard reputation, promote sales and build a corporate image. It meets a vital need in democratic society —the need to bridge the gulf which separate those having mutual interests and common causes.

The general goodwill, understanding and image building are the chief objectives of public relations and this is achieved through various public relations strategies. In order to make communication effective, the PR practitioner have to keep in view the message the media and the audience. Good public relations implies a sound a moral base, i.e., communication just be sincere and based on facts.

This book is designed to explain various strategies used by the new age PR practitioners for successful public relations. It describes the use of mass media and other tools of communication for achieving public relations objectives. It will familiarise readers with topics such as modern approaches to public relations, corporate public relations, implications of media in public relations, responsibilities of public relations, propagation of public relations, participatory public relations, media advocacy, ethical issues in public relations etc. For teachers, students and professionals in the field of public relations and mass communication, the book is destined to become a highly valuable reference tool.

Naval Prabhakar
Narendra Basu

Contents

Preface v

1. Introduction 1
2. Corporate Public Relations 26
3. Ethical Issues 46
4. Professional Responsibilities of Public Relations 71
5. Propagation of Public Relations 106
6. Participatory Public Relations 125
7. Implications of Media in Public Relations 168
8. NGOs and Media Advocacy 211
9. Modern Approach to Public Relations 248

Bibliography 293

Index 295

1

Introduction

There are some who say that Public Relations has always existed. They will point to cave drawings as an attempt to educate and inform future generations. The Bible, the Koran etc., are cited as early examples of written communication. As a profession, however, Public Relations is quite new. The person generally credited with founding modern-day public relations is Ivy Ledbetter Lee. Lee was retained as a press officer by the coal industry in the United States of America in 1906, at a time when the industry was attracting a huge amount of bad publicity. He was expected to be the 'mouthpiece' of the industry. A front man was needed and he was chosen.

However, as soon as he got the job, he issued a declaration of principles. The declaration really said that:

— He would deal only with the most senior level of management in the company;

— He must be told all of the facts (not just the version of the facts that the company wanted to issue);

— He alone would have the power to decide which facts, if any, were to be issued to the public; and, most importantly, he declared that:

— The public could not be ignored, or fooled, or put off by lies.

This statement of principles was revolutionary at the time. No one before had ever insisted that they would deal only with top management — after all, if you were only the mouthpiece of the company, it did not matter who gave you your instructions. It was also extraordinary that he insisted on being told all of the facts. Up to that time, there had been a belief that the press officer was there to tell a story to the public —not necessarily a true story.

By insisting on the facts, he was making sure that he never found himself in a position of having told lies to the public — a huge step. He was the first person to put respect for the public on the agenda. He insisted that he was not there to fool the public, to cover up, or to tell lies that sounded plausible. He was firmly of the opinion that the public had a right to be told the truth. He also believed that the public could not be ignored. No company could put its head down, and pretend that a disaster had not happened. The public had a right to be told what was going on — the bad news as well as the good.

Ledbetter Lee was the first person actually to bring journalists to the sight of a crash — a revolutionary move in those days. He believed that, instead of telling journalists a story, he should bring them, show them, tell them, let them take photographs and write the facts as they saw them. In the early days of his career, he was well regarded for his approach (in later years, he was known as Poison Ivy — but that's another story). After working with the coal industry, Ledbetter Lee went on to work for the railroad industry, and became an adviser to John D. Rockefeller Jnr.

Lee's entry into public relations was followed by that of another of the key influencers in the industry, Edward

Bernays. Bernays was a PR practitioner, well known for his use of propaganda and persuasion. He also taught the first course ever in public relations at New York University, and wrote Crystallizing Public Opinion, the first book on public relations. The practice of appointing press officers, and later public relations officers, spread. In Britain, after the Second World War, the government appointed a network of information officers — communications experts who would explain new concepts like pensions.

The first Public Relations (PR) post in a public company in Ireland was held by Ned Lawlor. He was appointed Public Relations Officer of the ESB (Electricity Supply Board) in the year of its foundation — 1927. He later went on to become the first president of the professional body, the Public Relations Institute of Ireland. The second PR person to be appointed to a similar position in Europe was Sir Stephen Tallents, who became public relations officer to the Empire Marketing Board in the United Kingdom (UK). The practice of national governments appointing PR people has continued to this day. Kuwait employed a PR firm to help it communicate with the world when Iraq invaded that country on 2 August 1990. More recently, every member state of the European Union (EU) employed communications experts to explain the Euro prior to its introduction in January 2002.

Before we look at definitions of public relations, we should first examine what it is not. Public relations is most often confused in the minds of the public with either propaganda or publicity. Propaganda is a deliberate effort to gain support for an opinion, creed or belief. Propaganda denies, or fails to recognise, the existence of, or merits in, alternative opinions. Propaganda makes an emotional appeal to the heart. Propagandists are prejudiced in favour of their topic, and therefore their concentration is on winning your support — not necessarily on being totally truthful with you.

Government press officers are often accused of acting as propagandists because they give only positive, pro-government answers to all questions. Public relations, by contrast, concentrates on truth. Where propaganda appeals to the heart, public relations is information — truth — which can be assessed by the mind. With any public relations activity, you are not trying to win people over to your cause blindly. You are trying to give them truthful information, which they may assess, and about which they may develop their own opinions.

Publicity is the other area most confused with public relations. What is publicity? Publicity is drawing attention to something by highlighting the issue, event or occasion in the media. You see it in newspapers and magazines and on television; you hear it on radio; you notice it in bus shelters and on poster sites. Publicity can be secured by buying advertising. It can also be secured by public relations techniques — by issuing a press release, pitching an idea for a feature article, calling a press conference, or organising a photo-call. Publicists, as a result, are often also referred to as press agents.

There are PR people who specialise as publicists. Max Clifford in the UK isprobably one of the best known, and he is extraordinarily good. In Ireland, GerryLundberg would undoubtedly be the best-known publicist. He has worked with allof the major theatre and film productions in Ireland, including Riverdance, My LeftFoot, The Field, In the Name of the Father, Some Mother's Son, Dancing at Lughnasa andWidow's Peak. Arts events in particular — film, theatre, poetry, visual arts — would not survive without the valuable work that publicists do. And it is hard to imagine an actor, actress, or performer of note who does not have their own publicist. Louis Walsh, manager of Boyzone, Westlife, Samantha Mumba and Six (among others), is also recognised as a great publicist, and is admiringly referred to by media as 'the spin king'.

Publicity sold copies of the painting, but public relations would have created an awareness of the antiques. Publicity can be secured by public relations means, but it is not the sole object of any public relations activity. It may be an end result (which is achieved from giving information), or it may be a selected tool used to reach a particular audience, but it is never the primary aim of any public relations campaign.

Misconceptions of PR Practitioners

In this section we will deal with some great misconceptions surrounding PR practioners— that people actually understand the kind of work we do. They do not. How many times have you heard someone say that their son or daughter is 'good with people' and should, therefore, go into public relations? Being good with people is an essential element of working for any company or industry, in any field. It is very difficult to work with people if you don't make an effort. If you make an effort, you become good with people.

There is also a belief that public relations people are generally young, female, blonde, charming, good-looking and often quite vacuous, and that they spend their days at press receptions, sipping champagne, talking to people, and, naturally, looking beautiful. Who on earth is going to employ you, and pay you money, to look beautiful while sipping champagne? There are many good-looking people in public relations. There are also many very ordinary-looking people, and some downright ugly-looking people. There are men and women, old and young, charming and narky, communicative and non-communicative (it's true), drinkers and pioneers. The same is true of any industry.

The misconceptions have probably developed for four reasons:

— No one really knows what we do, so people think they are working in PR, even when they are not. People working in customer care, product sampling, product demonstration, or customer hospitality will all tell you that they are 'in PR'. It is an industry which people want to be in, so they assign themselves the title.

— When PR people are photographed at client functions, it is usually the young, good-looking female ones who are photographed (but this is true of most media functions if the photographer is shooting for society pages or evening newspapers).

— Utterances by some of the people in the PR industry do not help! Lynn Franks' Californian PR company starts the working day 'by meeting around the kitchen table, lighting a candle, and holding hands for a blessing for the day, and sharing of what's going on for us individually'.

— The final reason for the misconception of our role is the way in which the press and media sometimes report PR people. We are either trivialised or stereotyped as baddies.

What matters in public relations is not how a person looks, but how well they can do their job. If you are dealing with clients and journalists, the last thing they want to do is talk to you about a company when you are nicely merry. PR practitioners may well have a drink when the function is over, but they have too much work to do during any function to be knocking back the champagne.

Professional PR Practitioner

If all of these commonly held misconceptions add up to a definition of what a PRperson is not, let us turn to look at what a PR person actually is. A good public relationspractitioner needs several qualities. At its broadest level, PR people need the following:

— *An understanding of communication processes*: They need to understand how messages are sent and received. They must be able to evaluate the response to a message, and to change and adapt their strategies so that messages are more clearly received and understood.

— *An understanding of the way the media works*: The media is often used as a means of conveying messages to the public. PR people need to understand the deadlines that different media work to, the formats in which information is most acceptable, the needs of print and broadcast journalists. They must understand the influence of the internet, the power of newsletters and magazines, and the value of oramedia (storytelling).

— *A keen understanding of the world of business*: Clients are very often drawn from the world of business. PR people need to understand the demands of business, the profit-making drive, the international repercussions of decisions, the value of trade unions, the implications of industrial relations disasters, the impact of decisions on share prices, and the power of shareholders.

On a personal level, there are certain qualities which undoubtedly help a PR practitioner:

— *A broad interest in the world of media*: Good PR practitioners are readers; they have the habit of reading, and are constantly developing their vocabulary. PR people ideally have a love of language, and take pride in how they would explain a concept.

— *An interest in what is happening in the media world*: PR people have a knowledge about which journalists write on certain issues. They have enquiring minds, constantly questioning the angles and perspectives that people take, and a curiosity about how a story was covered. They also have a broad interest in the issues of the day — be they national or foreign.

— *An interest in television*: The PR practitioner wants to know about the latest trends on TV (in particular, the growth of 'reality' television with programmes like Big Brother and 'Popstars'. Good PR people know the different TV personalities (and can, therefore, select the most appropriate person to act as a product endorser, or chair a meeting or introduce a video). They constantly look, enquiringly, at the way in which visuals on television portray a message, and wonder whose message they are receiving.

— *An interest in radio*: Good PR practitioners find it impossible to sit in a car and not listen to talk radio. They constantly study the interviewer, and the style of questioning. They wonder why this particular person is being interviewed at this time. They study how well the interview was conducted, and analyse whether or not the interviewee got their message across. They listen to things like the tone of voice used, the style of questions, and anger/remorse in someone's voice.

— *Curiosity and enthusiasm about the internet*: What is on the net? How is it presented? What messages are being transmitted? Who is using the net? Where are they coming from? Are there cultural differences?

— *An appreciation of films, theatre, music and the visual arts*: In essence, the good PR practitioner has an interest in all forms of media.

— *An interest in current affairs*: A good practitioner is someone who can debate the issues of the day. PR people need to know who are the key players — the Taoiseach, ministers, junior ministers, opposition spokespersons. They should be able to identify the policy differences between political parties. A good practitioner will study the influence of groups like An Taisce, the Trade Union Movement and women's groups. PR people will have an interest in changes introduced in the budget and will try to analyse the economic and social impact of those changes. They will study demographic changes, societal issues, trends in employment, and will know what is happening in the wider world. A good PR person follows the progress of bills through the Oireachtas; reads all of the pro- and anti-referendum (any referendum) literature; and studies racism, the collapse of rural areas, and the spending power of young people.

— *Excellent time management skills*: Public relations involves a lot of organisation —organising your own time, so that you can manage a number of clients in the same day, and organising functions like press receptions, press conferences, photo-calls, client meetings, and sponsorships. Without an ability to manage your time well, you will find that you are constantly busy, but achieving little.

— *Thoroughness*: A good PR person will be someone with the dedication to concentrate on the minor and major details of any public relations task, and see them through to fruition. There is no point in organising a function, and getting all of the big details right, only to fail because you did not concentrate on the minor details like organised car parking.

— *An ability to think strategically*: In addition to the ability to concentrate on the small things, a good PR person also needs to be a strategic thinker — to be capable of seeing the big picture. You need to know how your proposals will impact on the business you are advising, to see the developing trends and know how you might incorporate them into your proposals.

— *An ability to deal with people*: This quality is needed in every type of business. You will deal with many people every day — people you work with in the PR office, bank managers, journalists, clients, photographers, etc. You don't need to like them, but you must be able to deal honestly and effectively with them.

— *Honesty*: To work in public relations, you must be honest and trustworthy. You are dealing with sensitive, highly confidential information. You must be trusted both by clients and by the media. You will only be trusted and respected if you are honest.

— Imagination and creativity. There are many clients who will approach you with a brilliant idea which you are asked to implement — that is the easy end. There are also many clients who will approach you about their companies, which are perfectly ethical, financially sound, good companies — but they lack excitement. You are the person who needs the creativity and imagination to design something — of interest to the company and the general public — that will attract media attention.

Finally, all of these qualities are enhanced and developed by discussion with otherpractitioners. Opportunities for discussion usually arise through professional bodies. In Ireland, there are two organisations that represent professional public relations practitioners — the Public Relations Institute of Ireland, which represents all practitioners (and students) in the industry, and the Public Relations Consultants' Association (under the umbrella of the PRII), which represents consultancies. These bodies provide valuable professional and representative advice and offer opportunities to share information and interests with people of like mind.

Power of Brands

The power of brands is particularly obvious when you look at consumer purchases. People buy brand names they know and trust. A brand is bought for three main reasons — functional benefits (because it will do the job), psychic value (because it says something about the kind of person you are), and investment value.

Psychic value

The psychic value is created by the public relations and advertising people. Once wehave established the need for a car, and the functions it must have, we then look tothe psychic value of the product. We look for a car that says something about us andreflects our personality. We select the car (and often the colour) which best suits our'type' of person — flashy and sporty, conservative, executive, 4-wheel drive.

Look at the ways in which shampoos and perfumes/aftershave lotions are promoted. Any shampoo will wash your hair, but L'Oréal believes you should spend more 'because you're worth it'. Every bottle of perfume or aftershave is a bottle of smelly water, but you either buy cheap and cheerful, or you invest in seductive, expensive or sporty reflections (to your senses) of the kind of person you are. Psychic value is what PR people are really good at. We will build the lifestyle type to suit the product — the salespeople will then go and sell it to you.

Investment value

And finally, it must be a good investment — the car must actually hold its value; it must have trade-in value in a few years. The investment value of shampoos and lotions is that the investor believes in the product and therefore believes that a higher price is warranted because they are investing in themselves.

Attitudes and Opinions

Creating awareness is one thing, changing attitudes is another. Changing behaviour is the most difficult of all. Martin Higgins, interim chief executive of the Food Safety Promotions Board Do not be fooled into thinking that PR people always begin with a blank canvas —they do not. Very often, the job of the PR person is to change attitudes and opinions. This is a very challenging area of PR.

Virtually every decision in life is based on attitudes and opinions. Attitudes and opinions are formed by information, or lack of it. The more you know about a company, the clearer the mental image you develop of it. If the mental image is a good one, you are more inclined to buy the company's products, or give it the benefit of the doubt in times of crisis. Banks have been promoting pensions to young people for years. They are trying to change attitudes. People think of pensions as something they will need in their old age. Banks are trying to change attitudes and encourage people to take a pension when they are young, so that they will be protected and comfortable in their older years. So far, the response has been disappointing.

If you are seeking to convert negative to positive, you should be conscious of what you can realistically achieve. There were four main attitudes:

Negative	*Positive*
Hostility	Sympathy
Prejudice	Acceptance
Apathy	Interest
Ignorance	Knowledge

Hostility

If someone is hostile towards your company, it may be because of something that happened many years ago. The PR job is to try to inform that person of why it happened, how it happened, how the company dealt with the situation and how it has implemented changes which would prevent the same thing from ever happening again. What you are trying to achieve is sympathy. You do not expect that someone who is hostile to your company will suddenly become its biggest supporter, but you can expect them to become less hostile and slightly more sympathetic towards you if they fully understand the background and developments within the company.

Since the 1950s, the National Blood Transfusion Board had enjoyed a positive public profile. Donors at Pelican House (or mobile clinics) were plentiful, and the silver and gold pelican pins were worn by donors with pride. All that changed and the board became the object of hostility when the hepatitis C scandal broke in 1994. The eventual outcome was a public tribunal, called to investigate how an organ of the state was responsible for infecting its citizens.

The Blood Transfusion Board tried to change the hostility to sympathy by explaining that improved donor-screening processes had been introduced to ensure that this situation could never happen again. It changed its name to the Irish Blood Transfusion Service (IBTS) and moved from Pelican House to state-of-the-art headquarters at St James's Hospital. The Minister for Health appointed a new chairman, Michael McLoone, and the board probably believed that it had at least begun the process of change.

Prejudice

Prejudice is difficult to overcome because very few people understand why they are prejudiced against a person or a company or a brand. If, by giving people the information they need, you can convert their prejudice to acceptance, you have gone a long way down the road. The consumer who is prejudiced against your brand may never buy it, but, through exposure to public relations techniques, may come to accept that it is a good and reputable brand.

One of the best examples of a conversion from prejudice to acceptance was the Dublin Gas Company. Two people died in an explosion at an apartment complex called

Raglan House in Ballsbridge, Dublin, on 1 January 1987. It was several hours before the Dublin Gas Company issued its first public statement. The company was in receivership and the three-person PR department had been made redundant. External PR consultants had to be retained.

People in Dublin were hostile towards a company that did not seem to care. That hostility turned to prejudice when people, in vox-pop interviews, stated that they would not, under any circumstances, have gas in their homes. There was a prejudice against the product and the company that produced it, with many believing that it was unsafe.

To the company's credit, Bord Gáis, which had replaced Dublin Gas as the supplier,not only changed its internal systems, but also communicated the change so effectivelythat it is hard to imagine a home in Dublin that would now be prejudiced against thegas company. In fact, in 1990, by an extensive PR and advertising campaign (rememberthe gas company bears and the 50-50 cashback?) Bord Gáis succeeded in promotinggas as a lifestyle choice, which was environmentally friendly.

The company not onlyregained the confidence of consumers, but increased the sales of natural gas appliancesby 50 per cent that year. Who would want to deal with dirty grates and buckets of fuelif they could, instead, flick a switch and have the effect of a 'real' fire? It was a brilliantcome-back by the company, which had treated seriously the concerns of its customers.

Apathy

Apathy, essentially, is when people just don't care. They have no interest whatsoever inyour company. You need to convert that apathy to interest. This is one of the most difficultof all PR tasks. If someone simply doesn't care what happens to the environment, for example, or doesn't care who represents them at national or European level, how do you convert that total apathy to at least a mild level of interest?

Ignorance

Finally, you have to deal with ignorance — people simply may not know anything about your company and, because they know nothing, they cannot form any opinion about you, and are very reluctant to buy anything from you. By converting ignorance to knowledge, you are placing the person in a better position actually to make a decision. This is probably the easiest of the four attitudes to deal with, and the one on which companies spend large budgets. People are reluctant to buy from a company, or to invest in a brand, that they never heard of.

Companies are aware of that and consequently spend a large portion of their marketing budgets on research. As Bernadette Coyne, chief executive of Research Solutions has said: 'Research is information and information is power...if you don't know what people think of your brand or they think of the competitor's brand, you are disadvantaged'. As a result, not only marketing budgets but huge levels of PR resources are invested in telling the consumer, the investor and the influencer, about the company, its policies, its location, and its products

Dealing With Images

You will encounter many different images in your dealings with companies, organisations or charities. There are three, in particular, of which you should be conscious:

— Mirror Image

— Wish Image

— Multiple Image

The Mirror Image is what companies or individuals believe to be true of themselves.

The mirror image may, or may not, be true. It is not that companies are deliberatelytrying to mislead you, rather that they are deluding themselves. By research, you canestablish if you are dealing with a true or a mirror image. We are all guilty of selfdelusionin some way. How often have you seen a man or woman walking down the street, dressed in something 'hideous', which they believed was 'beautiful'? Too often! Yet they looked in the mirror that morning and believed that they looked absolutely wonderful. Companies are guilty of making exactly the same mistakes.

A Wish Image is what a company would like to be true of itself. It wishes that it could be the biggest in the field, or provide the very best quality service. The wish needs to be identified as such, and moved from being a wish to a goal that the company can attain and is taking steps towards achieving. Your job, as a communications expert, is to harness that goal and ensure that all of your communication strategies work to help the company achieve it.

A Multiple Image essentially refers to the fact that different publics have different images of the same company. People develop an image of a company based on their dealings with it: employees will have an image of the company based on their work experience; a retailer will have an image of a company based on the frequency of delivery and the billing method, etc. Each of the publics will have a different image of the company. It is your job, as a

PR person, to research and identify those images and use them in your communication with each of the groups.

Corporate Image is an expression much used today. We will look at corporate image and corporate identity in much greater detail later in this book. Finally, remember that what you are always trying to achieve, as a PR practitioner, is an accurate image of the company — an image that is a reasonable and accurate impression of an organisation and its products or services; an image that is based, most importantly, on the truth.

Public Relations Tools

Public Relations tools are stand-alone, camera or broadcast-ready materials that can be taken directly to media for publication or broadcast. They promote The American Legion, its programs, membership, latest advocacy campaigns and patriotic holidays. They are professionally produced by the national Public Relations commission office and are available free upon request in quantities needed by each post. Whether the PR tool is print or broadcast, space or time is left open for post contact information.

Every newspaper wants to publish the best, most professionally produced and eye-catching ad. Every electronic media wants the same for their medium. The Post Public Relations officer who can provide such a product enjoys a distinct advantage over others who may approach a media outlet with just notes scribbled on a piece of paper. Additionally, a professionally produced product is the end result of extensive research, editing and polishing of message points in compact, efficient packages.

American Legion PR media tools use advanced digital-editing techniques, professionally experienced talent, gifted writers, wide-ranging musical arrangements and sound effects. State-of-the-art graphics enhance television productions. The television spot available free to American Legion posts would typically cost more than $10, 000 to produce by a regional production facility. A professionally produced CD of a variety of 30-and 60-second public service announcements costs between $6, 000 and $10, 000, depending on studio time, talent fees, production technician hours, music license fees, CD packaging materials and complexity of different production elements.

American Legion media products are all produced at The American Legion 's own in-house, state-of-the-art, digital production facility at National Headquarters in Indianapolis. The Public Relations staff has worked professionally as writers, broadcasters and editors for both the Armed Forces Radio and Television Service and commercial stations and newspapers. Thus, PR materials can be developed and distributed on a continuous basis to meet the emerging issues of American Legion advocacy in addition to the perennial requirements of membership recruitment at no cost to the post.

The Message Is Local

All PR media tools are available free to American Legion posts, districts and departments. They are designed to maximize post community information. Radio and television spots can have post contact information added at the bottom of the screen; ad slicks can include post contact information, enabling readers, viewers and listeners to respond directly. While each PR media package includes some tools that provide national toll-free or online information, posts are encouraged to use the localization features for maximum community impact and response.

Variety

What is good for the goose may not necessarily be good for the gander. Some radio stations will readily air 60-second public service spots, while others may not accept any more than 30 seconds in length. The media products available for your use are designed to include a variety of sizes, lengths, formats and themes to accommodate nearly every type of print or broadcast station or cable system. The Public Relations officer can approach program and public-service directors armed with confidence and a full media tool kit to fit virtually any media requirement. Written copy for radio spots is included with each CD to enable stations that prefer to produce their own spots with their own announcers to use Legion materials.

Marketing

No PR media tool can be effective without getting it printed, broadcast or distributed. While mailings to local media with a cover letter signed by the Post Commander may work, that correspondence becomes just one of hundreds received by the station or newspaper. The tried-and-true, most successful method to get American Legion public service materials placed on a broadcast schedule, short of paid advertising, is through personal contact with station directors or editors who have cognizance over the schedule or layout of the publication.

Print Media

In this section you will find a background information sheet and significant dates in the history of The American Legion for use in developing a post media kit. Every post should have at least five media kits on the shelf, ready to be given to reporters who may show up at the post on short notice.

These materials should be augmented with another background information sheet listing the specific accomplishments of your post, including ongoing projects.

Use available blocks of white space on ad slicks to insert a contact name, post number and telephone number along with any specialized message that might be appropriate. While the ad slicks are designed primarily for use in publications, both internal Legion newsletters and commercial newspapers, creativity is key. For example, some posts have added contact information, made 1, 000 copies and placed them on the windshields of cars in shopping malls as handbills. Because most shoppers may not be veterans, this is a hit-and-miss technique. But if just five new members sign up, they can become active volunteers. Others have used the one column-sized ad slicks to reproduce and pass out as bookmarks at recruiting booths and area schools. Many post the slicks in windows of area businesses, the post office, train stations, etc.

Legion-specific clip art has been developed for use in post newsletters and advertising campaigns. Examples follow in this section. Art is updated periodically to reflect new themes of the organization as needed. Ideas for future development are always welcome.

Proclamations

Preparing a proposed proclamation for the mayor or county executive significantly increases the probability of having it signed and ready for use on an appropriate holiday. Positive news coverage can be garnered through use of proclamations to recognize veteran-oriented holidays and activities. On the following pages are suggested proclamations for The American Legion Birthday, Children &Youth month, Flag Day and Veterans Day. Using these as a guide, proclamations can be crafted for nearly any occasion or event. Try to get a draft to the mayor 's office at least 30 days prior to the event.

Media Campaign Kits

Complete media kits available from the National Public Relations office include a campaign-specific planning booklet, ad slicks, a television VHS spot video and a radio PSA spot CD. Ongoing campaign kits available free include:

— The Blue Star Service Banner and Flag Program

— "A Day to Remember, " annual remembrance program of the Sept. . 11, 2001, attack on America

— The American Legion Family Support Network

Campaign-specific media kits will be developed as needed to address breaking veteran and national security issues of importance to The American Legion. All are designed to facilitate ease of post participation with fill-in-the-blank news releases, letters, editorials, speeches, milestones, event planning, etc.

Radio Public Service Announcements

PR radio media tools include two formats: written and produced. Written copy included in Section 7 simply needs to be retyped, filling in the blanks with the appropriate local information and post contact, placed on post letterhead and marketed to area radio stations. The spots can then be read by the station 's on-air personalities when no commercials are sold for the time block. Additionally, a radio station may turn the copy over to the production department to add music, sound effects or multiple voices. The produced version would then be placed in digital memory for use during the normal PSA rotation within the station 's broadcast day.

Produced radio-spot packages are available on CD, including:

— Membership, including women and minority, recruiting

— American Legion Programs &Issues

— Patriotic Holidays

— Blue Star Service Banner

— "A Day to Remember "

Membership recruiting spots may or may not be accepted as public-service announcements by stations. Since a fee is charged for membership, some stations consider these spots advertising and require payment for broadcast. Section 8 will address the best methods of approaching this technique of reaching out to the community. Other stations will air The American Legion membership spots once they are aware that The American Legion is a tax-free 501(C)-19 veterans service and patriotic youth-oriented organization. As with all products, each CD contains spots with music beds at the end for post contact information.

Television Public Service Spots

The current inventory of television PSAs includes:

— Blue Star Service Banner (three 30-second PSAs)

— Membership (two 30-second PSAs)

— "A Day to Remember " ((one 30-second PSA)

Spots are provided on a VHS videotape or DVD for use in presenting to television stations and cable systems.

Professional BetaSP format tapes of higher quality can be sent directly to the broadcast facility by the National Public Relations office when a commitment to use is provided to the post. This service is free to the post or the broadcast facility.

Videos

— Good PR Equals Membership Success (Length: 15: 54)- American Legion Public Relations training video. It highlights all available PR tools and covers marketing, use of appropriate media, interview tips and basics of good post Public Relations strategy and planning. This is an excellent video for the entire post or the Public Relations committee.

— America 's Veterans (Length: 23: 00)- A video for school students about veterans, , Veterans Day and military service to America. Comes with a teacher 's guide and volunteer presenter 's outline.

— Reconnect (Length: 14: 16)- A motivational video for post showing on reaching out to younger, , active duty veterans.

— Others as required, including National Convention highlights, instructional videos on Legion programs, Protect Our Flag, etc. Contact National Public Relations for a complete listing.

PR Tools On The Internet

As media technology evolves, so does the ability of The American Legion to provide media tools directly to Legionnaires via the Internet. Nearly all American Legion media tools can be downloaded from www. legion. org.

Radio and television spots can be viewed or heard and immediately ordered online. Compact disc technology enables Legion radio spots to not only be top digital broadcast quality, ready for airing by radio stations, but also played on personal computers or "boom boxes. " Even American Legion ad slicks are available on CD, enabling post photos to be interchanged for those already on the slick and copy to be adjusted or edited for local requirements. As your American Legion national staff produces new media products, your suggestions and comments are always welcome. The PR staff stands ready to answer any questions on PR media tools or conducting your community Public Relations campaign.

2

Corporate Public Relations

Public relations creates awareness and support among an organization's constituents for its products, services, management views, intellectual capital and its distinct approach to doing business. It helps build credibility, manage risk, establish reputations and drive sales. As we practice it, public relations employs multiple marketing techniques: media relations, printed materials, speeches and seminars, surveys, CDs and DVDs, Internet-based strategies, direct response and special events.

INVESTOR RELATIONS

The *Makovsky Investor Relations Practice* assists companies in achieving the highest sustainable value for their securities, which reduces the cost of capital, facilitates acquisitions, incentivizes management and enhances shareholder value.

Branding

Brand power is the creation of value that goes beyond traditional measures such as sales and revenue. While often associated solely with products, branding brings value to business-to-business services, technology, health and other organizations, and can even impact the valuation of a company's equities. Public relations techniques that establish or enhance a brand are one of the hallmarks. For example, the top 10 global brands account for nearly $387 billion in value, equivalent to the entire gross domestic product of the Netherlands. Credible brands are one of the intangibles that create company value.

LITIGATION PUBLIC RELATIONS

When a high-profile case is in litigation, managing public advocacy in the media is critical to the final outcome. Litigation public relations can help to diminish and/or eliminate the business disruption caused by current or threatened legal actions, as well as influence the legal outcome in the company's best interests.

Crisis Management

Crises can be defining moments for an organization's reputation and often strike when a company seems least prepared. Most crises can be anticipated, and so we work with clients to plan response strategies before management finds itself in the whirlwind.

Visual Communications

Visual Communications Practice takes on the "word fatigue" battle. Whether creating a logo and visual identity system that gives visual clarity to a client's brand concept, or creating a corporate website that draws the clients' prospects in, the Visual Communications Practice integrates critical marketing functions into the total public relations package.

Corporate Public Relations Tools

Good public relations is more than just working with the media. It is a comprehensive strategy that involves creating a positive image of your company with your clients, employees and community. All of your materials and communications-printed materials, correspondence and discussions with clients, subcontractors and employees-contribute to your company's reputation and image. As a result, you should be careful that your are consistent in delivering your message in all that you say and do, via the printed and spoken word. Brochures, newsletters and Internet Web sites all can be used to enhance your firm's reputation.

Creating a newsletter

You may want to develop a corporate newsletter to send to business associates and clients. A corporate newsletter essentially becomes a marketing tool as it enables you to show off your company in your own words to potential clients and can raise your company's profile in the community. A good company newsletter can also put a human "face" behind your company. A letter from the company president or profiles of company employees in each issue can help your various "publics" get to know you better-publics who may be more inclined to use your services as a result. A company newsletter can also build morale and a "team" mindset in your most important asset-your employees.

Some things to consider:

Nameplate. The nameplate at the top of the front page sets the tone for the newsletter and should look appealing and professional. Don't overwhelm your front page with multiple fonts and complicated graphics. Sometimes simplicity works best. To get ideas, look at some newsletters that you think work well.

Size and length. Determine the size and format with which you are most comfortable, but keep in mind that most newsletters are printed in an 8 ½" x 11" or 11" x 17" size. Generally speaking, it is most cost effective to print a newsletter with page counts which are multiples of four. A basic sheet of press paper folds down into what printers call a "signature"-which consists of four or eight pages when folded down to size and trimmed. By containing your newsletter to one or more full signatures, you are assuring yourself of the most economical usage of the printer's press, which translates into lower reproduction costs. Other page counts can be used, but they may cost your extra.

Columns. You will generally want to divide your layouts into columns, which lend structure to the newsletter and make it easier to read. Again, look at some newsletters that you think have attractive layouts to determine whether they are divided into two, three, four, five or other column formats.

Fonts. Generally, for body text you will want to use serif fonts-fonts that have slight curvatures at the tops and bottoms-like Times Roman, New Baskerville (ABC Today type font), Palatino, or Bookman. For headlines, you will generally use a "sans serif" font such as Franklin Gothic or Helvetica. Body type should be 10-12 point sized.

Color. A full, four-color newsletter can be an expensive proposition. On the other hand, a plain black and white newsletter can look dull. You can bring a newsletter to life by adding one to two "spot" colors. Also, consider using a percentage of a color (such as 10 percent black or blue) behind boxed text -this is called a "screen"-to add more variety to your pages. However, make sure you run your photos in either black and white or full four-color. You don't want to make the mistake of running a photo in all red or all blue ink. Stick with black ink for text and photos and a second color for headlines, screens, logos, etc., and you'll be able to produce a sharp looking newsletter with no problems.

Photos. Use as many as you can in your newsletter to break up boring pages full of type. But make sure that the photos are of good quality so that they will reproduce well. A good camera is worthwhile investment. Photos really add to the interest value of your publication. Remember, people love to see pictures of themselves and their friends.

Computer software. Any format beyond one to two columns should be done in a desktop publishing software package, such as PageMaker or QuarkXPress. These packages allow you to custom design your publication with as many columns and graphic elements you want. Other software packages can be used, but PageMaker and Quark are the most frequently used by designers and printers. Additionally, computer and printing technology have evolved to the point that you can give your printer everything it needs on a computer disk; many printers no longer need "camera-ready" pages. Talk with your printer representative to determine how he or she would like to receive your publication.

Cultivating Relationships with Media

Relationships with the press should be cultivated over time. Perhaps some of the easiest connections to make are with editors of construction-related publications. These editors need you as much as you need them; the construction industry is their "beat," and they are always looking for good material to include in their publications. As a result, you may find them receptive to your ideas about projects you are working on, an innovative service, or awards won.

When you identify a construction-related publication that covers your area or your type of company, call or arrange a visit to introduce yourself to the editor and/or other publications staff. Get to know them. Then stay in touch. Give the editors a call from time to time or drop them a note, perhaps to update them on what you are doing or to comment on an article that has appeared in their publication. The main point is to form a mutually beneficial relationship that will strengthen over time.

There is a limit to the number of close editorial relationships you can maintain over an extended period of time, especially if you have responsibilities beyond press relations. Target those magazines that have the most significance to your communications goals. Don't play the advertising card. The quid pro quo school of PR is an insult to any editor who is serious about building an audience. It also brands the speaker as an amateur with dated notions about marketing communications.

Educate your target editors. Very few editors have expertise in the subjects they cover. Therefore, make education part of your relationship with target editors. Give them annual updates on what's happening in your company and your markets-technical changes, market share shifts, new applications, etc. This kind of information leads to article ideas and also stamps your company as a great reference for stories that touch on related subjects.

Meet face to face at least once a year. Use trade shows, association meetings, business travel to editors' cities, and similar occasions to cultivate relationships. Meals are better than meetings in the booth. If that's not possible, meet over a cup of coffee.

Follow up. Find a way to speak with your target editors at least once a year, if only for a few minutes. This can be a phone call. It can be mostly social, but make it a point to remind the editor of what you talked about at your last face-to-face meeting.

Have specific, realistic objectives. What do you want to get out of your relationships with editors? Have specific, long-term objectives for each magazine based on the type of material it publishes. Make sure your objectives are realistic. Don't let a friendship supersede business. Initiating and building relationships can be challenging. However, sometimes the most challenging situation for both a communicator and editor comes after a strong friendship develops. It's easy to spend an entire dinner talking sports, family and industry gossip and never get around to discussing the needs and interests of the magazine and your organization.

Similarly, sometimes communicators are reluctant to convey criticism or discuss negative subjects with a favored editor for fear of taking advantage of a friendship. These are business relationships and business friendships, and one of the main advantages to both parties is the foundation of straightforward communications.

Writing a feature article for possible publication in a local newspaper or trade journal can be a good way for you to garner some publicity for a specific project, employee or community service activity. Because many newspapers and trade journals accept "freelance" articles, you may find numerous opportunities to highlight a specific project or activity in depth. This not only showcases your company and the good work that it is doing, it also allows you to more effectively control the coverage that appears in the publication, because the article is written by you or someone on your staff.

Before submitting a feature article, find out if your targeted publication will accept articles. If so, find out what the word count and any other restrictions are so that your article fits into the parameters of the publication. Also, make sure you are familiar with the writing style of the publication: In order for an article to be accepted, it must be similar in tone and style. Perhaps you're not a writer. You can still "pitch" the idea of a feature article to editors. You can either write a short "pitch" letter or call to explain why the readers of your targeted publication would enjoy reading about your project/activity. Remember, editors, particularly editors of trade journals, are always looking for an interesting topic to feature in their publication.

Some tips for writing a feature:

— Your first paragraph should be interesting and be able to pique the reader's interest immediately. You want the reader to read the entire story, so you want to get them "hooked" right away.

— Your article should tell a story, with a clear beginning, middle and end. Try to center the story around an event that is inherently dramatic. For example, if you are working on a Habitat for Humanity project, make the main focus of your article the day(s) you spent building the project. This lends a narrative structure to your article and makes it more likely that readers will read the full article.

— Be sure to focus on people and include plenty of quotes. People like to read about other people and like to hear what they have to say. If you are working on a

Habitat for Humanity project, for instance, include quotes from project managers or employees working on the project.

— Be familiar with your target audience. Readers of a construction trade magazine will be looking for different things than readers of the local newspaper and will be more comfortable with construction-specific terminology.

Nine keys to effective media relations

1. *Develop solid relationships*. Take the time before a crisis strikes to get to know the key reporters in your local area and with the construction trade media who cover construction. There is no substitute for letting someone know that they can always pick up the phone and talk with you on a subject. Your company should have a list of key reporters with phone, fax and e-mail addresses if possible.

2. *Learn about the media work cycle*. Journalists have a tough job to do just like construction professionals. Theirs is a profession with its own ebb and flow. Be sure to learn about journalists' deadlines and to always meet them.

3. *Always be clear and truthful*. Don't try to be coy and deceptive with a journalist. It will always come back to haunt you.

4. *Don't go off the record*. If possible, always stay "on the record" when talking to a journalist. Going off the record only creates dilemmas for the journalist and potential problems for you. You don't have to offer any information that you do not want to offer, but you should never offer background information that you do not want to be attributed to you or your company.

5. *Relax.* A journalist will assume you have something to hide if you appear withdrawn or nervous, and this is an even more important consideration if you are doing a broadcast interview. Remember you are being given an opportunity to present your side of the story, so just relax and relay your thoughts.

6. *Stay on message.* Determine the key points you want to get across in the interview. Such as:

   "XYZ Construction has an outstanding record of safe, efficient, high-quality and cost-effective construction in this community. In addition, our employees are deeply involved in giving back to their community through volunteer service."

   Regardless of the interviewer's questions, continue to come back to these key points. Turn negative questions into positive responses. Never affirm the negative. If the journalist asks: "Does your firm have a disastrous safety record?", do not reply: "No, our firm does not have a disastrous safety record." In the public's mind, it will register that your spokesperson mouthed the words, "our firm" and "disastrous safety record."

7. *Prepare.* Anticipate the tough questions that the journalist may ask. Keep responses brief and positive. If there was a violation in the past, express regret and the steps that the firm put in place to eliminate this problem. Return quickly to your main point about the firm being a "better business" leader that is engaged in the local community.

8. *Be positive and enthusiastic.* Have an open face. You want to be perceived as the "good guy" that you are. Don't appear on television with a scowl on your face.

Don't sound anxious or annoyed when talking with a reporter over the phone.

9. *Reiterate your main point.* Be repetitive. Be repetitive. Be repetitive. When you want to make the point that your firm is a good firm, a solid member of the local community with a great track record, keep coming back to that point.

The news release is the main vehicle by which you disseminate information about your company. New hires, new projects and awards won are all good subject material for news releases. The editors and journalists you are trying to reach must sift through many releases from many organizations. You want to make sure that your release is read and not thrown on the discard pile. Your release should be written and formatted as professionally as possible. Some basic guidelines:

Your company should develop a letterhead template that includes the words "News Release" or "Press Release" at the top. This letterhead should also include the name of your key contact person, phone number, fax number and e-mail address.

Your "lead" sentence should have a news angle to hook the editor and keep him reading. Ideally, it should also include your company name and an action taken on that day or another date certain.

Avoid flowery prose and overuse of adjectives-the editors or reporters reading your release don't have time or inclination to try to figure out your point if it is not clear, and they are less likely to trust information that is clearly biased. Save the opinions for the quotes from your spokesperson.

Include plenty of quotes, because quotes are usually what journalists pick up from releases. The quote from your spokesperson is where you should include any information that is more opinion than fact.

Always be able to back up your statements and be sure of your facts. If you're not sure of something, leave it out.

Make sure you include contact information so the editor/journalist can call if they have more questions.

Journalists appreciate being kept informed. They need you as much as you need them. But remember: good media relations is based on relationships and trust. If you send out releases with erroneous information, you will lose credibility with the people you need to communicate your message to your "target audience."

Special events

Sometimes you can "create" news by staging a special event. Reporters are in the business of covering "news," and an open house, ribbon-cutting ceremony or special activity are all the types of events reporters tend to cover because they involve action and occasionally even drama. On the other hand, you don't want to throw the proverbial party to which no one comes. Make sure there is a reason for your event and that it has news value.

Media scholar Kathleen Hall Jamieson says news is "the report of an event that happened or was disclosed within the previous 24 hours and treats an issue of ongoing concern." This basic concept is the underpinning of what constitutes "news" and can inform your decisions about creating "happenings" likely to be covered by the press.

Some tips:

Planning is key. If every last detail is not thought about and planned, things could go wrong, which could prove embarrassing if members of the press are in attendance. Plan your event far enough in advance so that you have adequate time to make arrangements and attend to every detail.

Alert the press. Send out a media advisory or news release telling reporters the details about your event: when, where, who, etc. Or, if you are having a social event, send them an invitation. A few days before the event is to occur, call the reporters to remind them about the event and ask them if they plan to come. Make sure you include reporters and editors from publications that specialize in covering the construction industry.

Keep them happy. At the event, make sure you introduce yourself to the reporters in attendance and make sure they have everything they need to write their story. you may want to have a media sign in sheet that leaves room for reporters to write their address and phone number. That way, you can reach them after the event if you need to. If there is food at your event, make sure the reporters are fed.

Writing a letter to the editor

The philosophy behind your newspaper's letter-to-the-editor page can vary dramatically. The key variable is the size of the paper. Some editors see this page as a community bulletin board on which all sorts of opinions may be posted. For example, you might see a letter from a homeowner complaining about a recent county commission vote, even if the newspaper never covered the commission. This wide-open policy is typically found at smaller papers, where there can be more of a challenge to fill space.

A more common approach is the one taken by many mid-size to large newspapers. These papers receive many potential letters to the editor each day. For the editors of these larger papers, relevance is the key consideration. They only print letters to the editor that offer feedback, criticism or praise for stories and opinion columns that have recently appeared in their paper. You should read the letters to the editor that are frequently printed in your local newspapers. This is the single best indicator of the style that works with the editors of those papers. Once you determine the best approach, then you're ready to begin.

Read the publication regularly. You need to be familiar with the publication to be able to comment intelligently about it in a letter to the editor. Know what you're writing about. If you criticize a column, you need to be sure you are factually correct. The same holds true for praise or additional observations.

Watch your tone. There are times when an indignant approach may work, but usually a reasoned and respectful tone is best. You can be direct and critical without being unprofessional. If you are writing representing ABC you want to be professional. Furthermore, this is a wiser approach since you will likely in the future need to work with the journalist whose story you are critiquing.

Be sure you're clear on word-count requirements. All papers have either a specific or general word-count limit on letters to the editor. Call ahead to be sure, rather than risk having a good letter rejected because it's too long-or too short.

Cite the story you are responding to at the beginning of your letter. Usually it is best to refer to the columnist, story title and date of the story in your opening paragraph.

Write and rewrite. Often it is the best written pieces that are run.

Have someone look over the piece for any grammatical errors, typos, punctuation errors, etc.

Ask for deadlines and how the paper would like to receive your piece. In most cases, it is best to fax your letter, and then follow up to be certain it was received.

Provide information on how you can be reached. Most papers will follow up with you directly to verify you wrote the piece before they run it. Include your daytime telephone number when you send your letter to the newspaper. Some newspapers require both a home a business telephone number for any letters submitted.

Follow up. If you haven't heard anything after a few days, give the editor a call. Inquire politely.

Don't get discouraged if you don't get into the paper. Continue to send letters on a variety of topics which affect ABC and merit shop construction. Eventually your persistence will pay off. In some cases, you may decide to write a full-blown opinion editorial.

Most of the previous points hold true for op-eds as well. Often it is more challenging to get an opinion editorial into a newspaper than a letter to the editor. The goal of the op-ed page is to give writers from outside the newspaper staff an opportunity to voice their opinions on matters of community/public interest. Opinion editorials are usually longer than letters to the editor. Additionally, they do not necessarily need to be in response to a particular story run by the newspaper in which they appear. They are simply the writer's opinion on a particular issue. The best opinion editorials are filled with factual data supporting an argument. They are written like a good news story, with the lead at the beginning, the body of supporting evidence in the middle and a strong conclusion encouraging readers to take a particular course of action at the end.

Crisis Communication

What do you do when the worst happens and an accident or other crisis occurs at one of your jobsites? If not handled properly, the reputation of your company could be at stake. However, with proper planning and an appropriate response, a crisis doesn't necessarily mean disaster in terms of your standing in the community and with your clients. The key is to develop a plan for responding to a crisis before the crisis occurs. In your planning process, try to consider several scenarios in which a crisis could occur and devise a plan to respond to each one.

Decide who will be the spokesperson, what you will say, what you will do. This will enable you to respond quickly and appropriately when faced with a volatile situation. Realize that during a crisis, the media could be either your friend or foe, depending largely on how you respond and how you treat them. Try to build relationships with local journalists so they know you and your company long before a crisis occurs. That way, when the unexpected happens, a relationship already will be established. They will know your company and know what you do, and their story will likely reflect that.

If a crisis does occur:

Appoint one individual to serve as a spokesperson. Having one spokesperson prevents conflicting messages from being communicated to the media and avoids confusion in identifying who has the authority to say what. Be honest and forthright in what you say. It is better to acknowledge that a mistake has been made and explain what you are doing to address the problem than to try to cover it up. If you are not sure of something or don't know the answer, say so.

Do not say "No comment." It makes you look evasive and defensive and breeds hostility among reporters. If you cannot comment on something, explain why.

Make sure all key personnel are able to stay in touch via cellular phone at all times and give reporters a way to reach your spokesperson after hours.

Communications Advice

Conversation is the root of all oral communications. The goal of communications is to implant in my mind what's in your mind. And that is done best when you talk to me. The burden of the effort is on the communicator. Don't ever forget that. Moving your mouth and saying words in a common language isn't enough. The one who appears to be reasonable, sensible, trying to be reassuring usually wins.

Remember your goal is to be liked. You want to win over the other people in your audience. Think of Mike Wallace from "60 Minutes." When the person he's interviewing looks shady, evasive, unlikable, you root for Wallace. You want him to burst that awful person's balloon. When the person he's interviewing looks pleasant, likeable and in control, you tend to wonder why he's so rotten to that nice person.

Use the techniques to make yourself that likeable person everyone is rooting for. And, remember, practice makes perfect. Practice with your colleagues, your family, your neighbors and your coworkers. See how warmly people react to the smile, the open face, the gesture and eye contact. Put these new skills to work the next time you meet a stranger. Open your face, smile and say "Good morning!" You'll probably make that stranger's day. You'll probably get such a pleasant response, you'll make your own day too.

When you're called upon to speak to the media or before an audience, make it a point to be the same human being you are when you talk to your neighbors and friends. Don't be surprised when you're met with equal warmth and enthusiasm.

Tips for Media Interviews

Not many years ago, few people were likely to be interviewed by the media. Times have changed. With more and more cable stations, "news" magazine shows, radio talk shows and trade professional journals, we've all become fair game. Most people have a natural fear of the unknown when it comes to media interviews. Training will help you become more comfortable with the role of interviewee. But for now let's go over some basics:

Most journalists are decent, honorable people. They want you to do well. Some "tabloid" reporters may not, but don't let them bait you into a fight. Use them to reach your audience. You'll reach your audience if you're likeable. We listen to people we like. We want to believe people we like. But it's hard to like someone who frowns and snaps at a reporter, even in response to an attack. Once you reach your audience, through being likeable, you want to project competence. It doesn't matter how brilliant you are if your audience doesn't perceive you that way.

So let's look at some Dos and Don'ts that will help your audience like you and trust your information. Your goal is to be so good and interesting that they'll put your interview on the air or write a glowing article. Next best is to be so good that they decide not to use the interview. The damaging scenario is that you're terrible and you show it. That won't happen if you follow these Dos and Don'ts.

Dos,

— Prepare, practice, rehearse
— Dress appropriately: long-sleeved shirts and over- the-calf socks for men; clothes that cover cleavage, upper arms and thighs for women
— Accept an offer of make-up at the studio
— Breathe deeply, rhythmically, from the diaphragm
— Open your face: raise your eyebrows to create horizontal lines in your brow
— Let hands fall loosely at your sides
— Smile when appropriate
— Sit correctly: erect, leaning slightly forward, knees together
— Gesture when appropriate
— *Be honest*: admit it when you don't know the answer; admit it if an obvious problem exists
— *Pause*: think, maintain eye contact, remain silent (except on radio and telephone).
— *Be positive*: say what you DO, not what you don't do
— Be proud of yourself and your organization
— *Be understandable*: simple, brief, clear, concise
— *Be quotable and memorable*: tell stories, use examples
— Look at the person who's speaking
— Look at the person whose question you're answering
— Vary the pitch and rate of your speech

— Stop talking when you've answered the question

— Be informative, educate ñ that's why you're there!

Don't

— Wing it.

— Wear or do anything that calls attention to itself and away from your message.

— Allow yourself to be placed with the sun in your eyes.

— Frown or close your face.

— Maintain a neutral, expressionless face.

— Lock yourself into positions like the fig leaf (hands grasped together in front of mid-section) hands crossed over chest or hands thrust into pockets.

— Slouch, fidget or swivel in your chair.

— Repeat negatives, tell us what you don't do or make denials

— Lose your cool or get angry

— Say "no comment." If you can't comment, explain why.

— Be pompous by trying to look professional or using jargon or "scholarly" words and language.

— Keep talking just because the microphone is still in your face.

— Talk to the camera unless you're instructed.

— Look at the TV monitor.

— Be shocked. Expect loaded questions and rigged statements.

— Shout, or even speak loudly (let the microphone do its job).

— Speak in a monotone.

3

Ethical Issues

Public relations activities of influence — and that includes such simple activities as communications meant to educate — are being closely scrutinized. At a time when the public relations profession is most needed, at a time when institutions and values are being attacked from all sides.

"Spin doctors," "PR ploy," "PR maneuver," "PR effort" — these denigrating epithets abound in the news media and in normal, daily conversations between normal, educated citizens. More and more, people are paying attention to what public relations professionals are doing. And more and more, they're calling on actions they consider unethical. Let's face it, folks. The "ethics police" are here. They're outside your door, they're on the street, they're in their homes, they're in front of their TV sets, they're in their cars listening to their radios . . . why, they're even in your own offices.

Every minute of the day, every day of the year, know that you are being watched. The ethics police are looking hard for conflicts of interest, they're looking hard for improprieties, they're watching for a slip-up, they're itching for a fight, they're waiting to pounce. But you know what? They have every right to. After all, public relations is an advocacy profession. Our ultimate goal is to influence public opinion. Our ultimate objective is to get people to take positive action on behalf of our client, organization or cause. And that in itself is controversial.

Challenges of Public Relations Profession

From simple turn-of-the-century press agentry, the public relations profession has assembled an impressive arsenal of strategies and tactics that influence. If it can be communicated, we're right there. If it can't be communicated, you can be sure that we'll find a way. From print, through radio, through television, through the Internet, public relations professionals have been in the forefront of usage. It's quite a powerful position we hold. And because of this power, the public relations profession faces tremendous challenges:

— *Misleading Information*: We're counted on and trusted to provide accurate information to our publics. It's so easy to send out — on purpose — incorrect information designed to lead them astray. Does "Sell the sizzle, not the steak" sound familiar?

— *Influence of Management Actions*: If we have won the ear of our CEOs, then we are remarkably well-positioned to influence the way our client, company or organization operates. How we exert this power is cause for concern.

— *Promotion of Inferior Products*: How ethical is to promote products made by our company that we know are inferior — products that we know are unsafe, or of poor quality, or will be used illegally?

— *Discrimination*: As elementary as this may sound, we are still constantly faced with issues of discrimination — religion, appearance, physical disability, sexual orientation, age, race, or gender.

— *Destruction*: Public relations professionals today are taking sides in the use of national parks, the issue of endangered species protection vs the right of American citizens to find work, destruction of rainforests vs the desire of underdeveloped countries to improve their standards of living.

— *Pay Inequities*: Do men still make more than women in equivalent jobs? Is there still a glass ceiling in American business? In the public relations profession? The debate rages on.

— *Gain at Expense of Others*: To the victor belong the spoils, the Law of the Jungle, only the strongest will survive, nice guys finish last, the "New Golden Rule" (The one with the gold, rules).

— *Political Influence*: Does money still buy influence in politics? Should public relations professionals use Political Action Committees — better known as PACs — to gain influence with elected officials through economic support? It happens all the time. Is it ethical? Or is it just good business?

— *Promotion of US Products*: In many foreign countries, American companies are promoting and selling products deemed unsuitable for use in the USA (e.g., pesticides, herbicides). And, they are pulling out all the stops in the tobacco industry to sell cigarettes in Asia. Again, ethical? Or just good business?

When it's all said and done, what you do in your own particular situations will be judged by your bosses, by yourself, and by the general public in the court of public opinion. Whatever you do, whatever your choices are, choose well, and represent yourself well in this court of public opinion, because . . . you will be judged. And as public relations practitioners, you represent the entire profession. How you respond to your particular ethical dilemma will invariably affect your colleagues' livelihood.

Ethics Systems

Before we talk about some solutions and present some thoughts that will help you, let's examine ethics itself. The question of what is right and what is wrong is not an easy one. We all have our personal ethical standards; each of ours is different. Let's begin with a look at three basic ethical systems: Deontology, teleology, and Aristotle's Golden Mean.

— *Deontology*: This system is duty-based and relies on moral obligation. Deontological ethics says that all actions are inherently right or wrong. This system depends on the inner-based, self-discipline of each individual public relations practitioner, and because we are all human, and of different environmental backgrounds, it changes from person to person, depending on their own cultural and traditional biases.

— *Teleology*: This system is outcome-based. Teleological ethicists believe that "the ends justify the means." While this system has had its detractors, there is considerable historical precedence, and deserves extended discussion.

Christianity, for example, began with one man battling what he considered corrupt religion. Jesus Christ used what we today would call classic public relations techniques: He used the two-step flow theory of communication, He did a lot of public appearances, He staged special events, He identified and targeted specific audiences, and He adapted His message to each audience. In the case of Christianity, did the ends justify the means?

Another good example is the American Revolution. Did you know that generally speaking, the American colonists were not terribly unhappy with British rule? It took a small cadre of about a dozen patriots to convince them. Like Christ before them, they used classic public relations tactics: Publications, public appearances, triggering events such as the Boston Massacre, special demonstrations such as the Boston Tea Party, eloquent speakers, and simple slogans: "Taxation without representation is tyranny!" "Don't tread on me!"

Today, the techniques being used by Greenpeace bear watching. Only history will tell if their activities of civil disobedience as once described by Henry David Thoreau bring changes for the better good in the end.

In the TV series, Capt. Janeway recalls the "Double Effect Principle on Assisted Suicide": "An action that has the principle effect of relieving suffering may be ethically justified, even through the same action has the secondary effect of possibly causing death." Fiction, true, but interesting none-the-less.

Public relations professionals have a problem. As counselors, we need to know everything about a company, organization or cause. This is indisputable. We cannot fulfil our responsibilities without this knowledge. And yet, because of our loyalties to our employer or client, we must keep it confidential. No matter how open and candid we wish to be, there are some things (e.g., trade secrets, business strategies, employee information) that must be kept in confidence.

And yet, as the conscience of business, as the company's liaison with the public, we have a duty and obligation to reveal it to the public, even if we could lose our job or hurt others — including our own dear family members — in the process.

Which brings us to a defining question for public relations practitioners: "What is the threshold beyond which an advocate may not ethically go? Is there some point at which we can say "It is ethical for me to do this one thing, but if I change this one particular element a mere 0.01%, then it becomes unethical"? Where then is the line beyond which public relations counselors are morally obligated to sacrifice self and client for a larger social good? And if such a line exists, then how to we know when we've crossed it?

If you belong to a professional organization—communications/public relations-related or otherwise—make sure it has an ethics code with teeth, one that obligates its members to abide by, upon pain of expulsion. Live by its code. Finally, if you are in a counselor's position, or any position of influence in your organization, make sure you are included whenever organizational policies are reviewed and formulated.

There are no simple solutions in the public relations ethics. Wending your way through the ethical minefield requires continual monitoring of current social conditions, continuous two-way communication with all stakeholders, constant monitoring of organizational's behavior vis-a-vis its policies, an increased awareness among public relations professionals and management that ethical performance makes for long range stability, and a never-ending effort to achieve ethical performance in order to achieve effective public relationships.

In public relations ethics, there are no right or wrong answers. There are only courageous decisions. In public relations, you need to take every risk you can. It is unethical for a public relations professional to fear failure. In public relations — as in life — we need to make courageous decisions, day-in and day-out.

In their book, *Public Relations Ethics,* Philip Seib and Kathy Fitzpatrick talked about five duties of public relations professionals. These are the 5 Masters — self, client, employer, profession and society. When faced with an ethical dilemma, look first within yourself at your own values. These will guide decisions based on what you truly believe is right or wrong.

The client is generally the first loyalty beyond self (you can substitute the word "organization" if you don't do work for clients). Decide if you are doing work for the client or organization, or if it's for the "cause" that they represent. Remember—as long as you work for a client, there are some confidences that you must keep. Ask yourself, "Knowing what I know, can I represent the client, do what has to be done, and still sleep well at night?" Your employer signs your paycheck. No work, no public relations ethics decisions. It's as easy as that. But if you knowingly allow harmful work to continue, you'll be violating your duty to the public, which many would agree takes precedence over duty to employer. Ask yourself, "Is the work I'm being asked to do harmful to the public?"

As a public relations professional, you are obligated to support your colleagues. You are obligated to be responsible to your peers. To produce unprofessional work is unethical. Allowing others to produce unprofessional work borders on being unethical. Ask yourself, "Is what I'm about to do professional? Is it what my role models would do?" Finally, society is the key component to ethical public relations decisions. We must serve the public interest. This particular master takes precedence over all the others, including self. Ask yourself, "Will my decision benefit society, even if I hurt myself, my client, my employer or my profession?"

Reputational Tracking

"Reputation" reached its heights as a buzz word in the late 1990s, and established itself as a relevant business and public relations strategy. This has not changed, especially in these times of crisis, when companies need as much sway with their stake holders as they can muster. Those with good reputations fare much better than those without. Before people began talking about reputation, there used to be talk of a "bank of good will" that was supposed to be replenished to overflowing, and drawn upon in times of dire need. This "bank" was never fully validated, primarily because "good will" was something that was difficult to quantify.

Decades of good service and good will toward the public could never mitigate the effects of a single disaster. What can sustain a company, however, is reputation. When an organization has a reputation of being responsive and fair-minded, willing to change with the times, and genuinely caring of its stakeholders, people know it. In difficult times, a company's hard-earned reputation will see it through crises.

A good reputation is the result of being distinctive, focused, consistent, identifiable and transparent. Reputation is measurable. It can be indexed, it can be quantified, and it can be given value. This is done through a process called "reputational tracking," which involves examining what the public expects of the company vis-à-vis what the public's perception is of the organization's performance.

What areas can be indexed and measured? Ethical leadership, industry issues, corporate citizenship, business leadership, stock performance, among others. The relative ranking may change from time to time, but the essential areas are constant. Reputational tracking begins by identifying essential elements of what identified audiences believe makes up a good reputation, and how important they are in relation to the others. These elements that can influence change a company's reputation are then tracked, trends are identified, and potential or occurring changes in reputation can be predicted.

According to the Reputation Institute, measurable elements include:

— *Emotional appeal*: Admiration and respect

— *Products and services*: Quality, value, reliability, innovation

— *Financial performance*: Profitability, willingness to risk

— *Vision and leadership*: Direction and philosophy

— *Workplace environment*: Management, quality of employees

— *Social responsibility*: Good citizenship

Through the tracking process, which should involve a number of research methodologies, unrealistic public expectations may be uncovered, information as valuable as the comparison itself. It may also discover that the public does not fully understand what the organization can or cannot do – again information of great value.

Reputational competition is pretty much a driving force in today's economy. If companies are in tune with their customers' expectations, and if they meet those expectations, they will earn a good name and reputation. The result is a competitive advantage, a direct impact on the bottom line. A good reputation is the fuel that makes an organization competitive.

Effective Public Service Announcements (PSAs)

The first thing you should know is that radio and TV stations are obligated to run PSAs. The Federal Communications Commission renews their broadcast licenses only if they have demonstrated a fine record of public service. Broadcasters therefore need a thick file with thank-you letters praising the fine work they're doing on the community's behalf. Yes, they are obligated to run PSAs. But they are not obligated to run your's. Let's just talk about radio, if only because TV PSAs present a whole new set of problems to overcome and quite frankly.

There are six rules to writing effective PSAs:

1. Compel the audience to listen.
2. Empower the listener to take responsibility.
3. Make every word count.
4. Play with the listener's emotions.
5. Register the name of your organization.
6. Call for action.

Compel the audience to listen

Unless they listen, they ain't a-gonna hear your message and plea. That's why you have to make them listen. Think of your own radio-listening habits. Exactly what is it that compels you to listen to a commercial, or a talk show, or an announcement, or anything for that matter? Does it entertain? Probably. Does it give you information that you need? Possibly. Does it make you recall your own experiences? Maybe. Does it make you want to do something? Very likely. Every good radio experience does one or more of these things.

But there's one thing great radio experiences have in common — they involve you to the very fiber of your soul. They get you talking back to the radio. They get you pounding your steering wheel in laughter while you're stuck in rush-hour traffic. They bring tears to your eyes with their heart-felt messages. They compel you to listen. You simply cannot turn away. And that's what you need to do. Relate to their own lives. Show them why they need your organization or service. Compel them to listen.

Hard to do? Of course it is. Nobody said writing PSAs was easy. If you're going to be satisfied with simple meeting announcements and innocuous messages, then go ahead and take the easy route. But if you want your PSAs to work, you need to work at it until you sweat blood.

Empower the listener

The effective, successful PSAs are the ones that empower the listener. They give the listener the right to take responsibility. They validate the listener's decision to take action. In other words, they send a message to the listener that says "You have the right, the duty, and the responsibility to take charge of the situation and do something about it." One of the best examples of empowerment is the anti-drunk driving campaign. The original campaign focused on why people shouldn't drink and drive. It showed twisted automobiles at accident scenes, ambulances, police, dark rain-slicked streets, flashing light and sirens. The campaign didn't work. DUI arrests continued to rise.

They revamped the campaign strategy by taking responsibility away from the driver and giving it to the passengers. The result was the "Good Friends Don't Let Friends Drive Drunk" campaign. It worked. What the PSAs did was empower us. It gave us the right to take the keys away from friends who've had too much to drink. And, it not only gave us the right to save their lives, it also made us responsible for our friends' actions. It did this — not by preaching to us, but by showing us the painful process people go through when deciding whether or not to intervene in their friends' lives.

What the campaign showed was that we should not focus on the negative, but on the positive. Empower your listener. Give the listener the right, the duty, and the responsibility to help your cause.

Make every word count

Thirty seconds can be a long time (like when you're late and stuck at a traffic light, or when the dentist has a drill inserted in your mouth, or when you're about to give a speech), but not when you're trying to persuade someone to do something for you. There aren't a helluva lot of words you can fit into a 30-second PSA, so it behooves you to make every word count. Every word has a purpose. Every word must be focused on one thing and one thing only — to sell your idea or suggestion.

Follwing are some hints for how to tighten up your writing. First, get rid of certain words. Whenever possible, eliminate the word "that." Go through your copy and you'll find most of your "thats" are unnecessary. Second, change the word "get" into an action verb that paints pictures, words such as "earn," or "secure," or "acquire." Third, eliminate as many prepositional phrases as possible. That will tighten up your writing considerably. Instead of saying "Pat Jones, president of the Humane Society of Clarksville," say "Clarksville Humane Society President Pat Jones" and you've eliminated three words. Consider the word "of" to be an enemy of mankind.

Fourth, try to find the "perfect word," but don't become obsessed with it. The perfect word must be understandable by the vast majority of listeners. There is a local radio commercial by a law firm that uses the word "egregious." Unless you use the word a lot, you probably don't know that it means "deplorable," "flagrant," "glaring," "infamous," "notorious," or "outrageous." But chances are you have heard of those other synomyms, those other words that are just as colorful but that make a lot more sense to you.

Fifth, if at all possible, stick to one idea. Concentrate on one main persuasive thrust. Otherwise, you'll confuse the listener. Sixth, use humor sparingly in PSAs. You won't often find the perfect humor that will influence opinion and spark behavior favorable to your organization or cause. Improperly used, humor can appear cruel and insensitive. Improperly used, it can ruin your campaign. Finally, don't be afraid to break all the grammar rules you learned in school. This is radio, this is excitement, this is short attention span, this is 30-seconds. If it takes broken sentences, then so-be-it. If it takes mispronunciations, then so-be-it. If it means you talk in sentence fragments, then so-be-it. Break the rules if you have to, but ONLY if you HAVE to.

Play with emotions

Grab'em by the head, and they'll follow you; but, their eyes and heart will be focusing elsewhere. Grab'em by the heart, and you've got them forever in your clutches. Make them feel the pain. Make them wipe away the tears. Make their hearts glow with pride. Make them remember good times. Make them think about their loved ones. Make them taste the homey goodness of the beef stew that's been sitting on the back burner for hours while freshly baked bread spreads its aroma around the house.

You can either appeal to the listener's five basic needs (shelter, food, clothing, appreciation or love, and vanity) to evoke a gut-wrenching reaction, or you can appeal to their wants, which are unlimited. Generally speaking, if you want something, chances are others will want it too. Use your intuition; you may be surprised at how universal your wants are. Select a persuasive appeal. Here are 11 basic psychological appeals: sensory, appetite, security, acquisition, well-being, attractiveness, threat, humor, convenience, curiosity and ego. Just make sure your appeals are honestly based. Don't overpromise. It may increase the response, but disappointment will result in a devastating loss of credibility.

Register the name

Do it early, and do it often as possible. Establish the name and repeat it. The general rule of thumb is once for a 10- or 15-second PSA, at least twice for a 30-second spot, and at least three times for a 60-second PSA.

Call for action

Finally, don't forget the call to action. It's a sales technique.

If you don't ask for help — specific help — people won't be obliged, they won't feel empowered, to do something for you. Remember, the whole purpose of the PSA is to elicit a specific behavioral action. In other words, there is something — a precise action — that you want the listener to do. Too often, an organization's strategy is to educate people about the mission, objectives and activities of the organization. This is not only useless, it is a stupid waste of time. At the risk of sounding cynical, most people don't care what an organization believes in. And generally speaking, if it doesn't affect them directly, they also don't care what an organization does.

What they do care about is how the action you're asking them to take will help make society better, and especially how it will help them personally. You need to have provided those reasons earlier. If you've done that, then now is the time to ask for a specific action on their part. This is the payoff. If they don't do what you want them to do, if they don't do it in the numbers you need to make your campaign succeed, then something went wrong.

Strategic Roles

Since its early development in the late 19th Century, the public relations function has evolved the roles that it plays in society. Throughout the years, four basic roles that define implementation of public relations strategy have emerged: Educator, facilitator, persuader, and partner. Each does not exist exclusive of the others, each can be used in combination with the other three, and yet each can be effective in its own right.

By presenting unbiased facts – using neutral language in an unbiased setting – the public relations professional relies on the public's interpretation of these facts to arrive at appropriate and sensible conclusions. The messages (and the media used) themselves do not present conclusions, and do not in any way attempt to influence the target public. They may, however, present a variety of alternate solutions and allow the public to make up its own mind.

Government agencies (via public information officers) utilize this strategy to a large degree, in trying to avoid the perception that they are using public funds to influence public opinion. This role is effective only if one is certain that providing the information will result in favorable action; education in itself is not a desirable end. It is one-way, without a call for action, and results cannot be predicted. When a public is predisposed to act in a certain way, the public relations practitioner is positioned to help move them along in the process.

As a facilitator (someone who makes the process easier), the practitioner provides the public with resources they can use – e.g., "Q&A's," postage-paid return envelopes, pamphlets, the use of interactive websites, "How To's," form letters, directional billboards, money, logistical and material support. This facilitative strategy is more effective than the pure educator strategy, in that it gives people the tools it wants or needs to take a behavioral action. It can provide that one additional little "push" that will overcome the inertia in a potential supporter or participant.

Although the results become a little more predictable (at least the practitioner has stacked the deck in his/her favor), it is still one-way, there is no definitive call for action, and there is a fair amount of uncertainty over the outcome.

In the persuader role, the kid gloves are removed. This is the advocacy mode whereby public relations appeals to the values and emotions of its target publics. Information is presented – quite frankly – in a biased manner, designed to convert, change, or conserve the public's attitudes and expressed opinions to the organizations' favor. Information presented may be selective. That is, both sides of the story may not be presented. Language certainly is not neutral, but will reflect from the organization's point of view why it is important for it to be involved in the situation.

There is – and always will be – controversy over public relations' role as persuaders. Whether it's called the "engineering of consent" (coined by E.L. Bernays), or "spinning" (a favorite of political animals), persuasion will have its detractors. Suffice to say that persuasion is and always has been a part of society, especially in the United States. More effective than educational messages or facilitative tools, persuasive messages provide a call for action, either directly or indirectly. The persuader role, although basically one-way, does use feedback to determine how best to reach the public emotionally and logically.

The last role is that of partner. It is the only purely two-way symmetrically oriented role played by public relations professionals. It is also the most difficult, time-consuming and painful, in that the organization must work cooperatively with outside groups – specifically community and other stakeholders. In a partnership strategy, communications between the organization and its publics transcends all levels, reflecting a cooperative willingness among all concerned, not only to define problems but to present, debate and adopt solutions amenable to everybody.

Information is openly exchanged, common goals are adopted, tasks and responsibility are shared. The organization listens, and to the extent that it can, makes its policies from the joint collaboration. Because of this interdependence, the organization and its publics become one. Public relations, through its position of power in the organization, makes this partnership possible.

Use of Colour

We don't live in a black and white world consisting merely of light, darkness and tones of gray. Rather, our world is vibrant and alive with millions of colors that we often take for granted. We need to take greater notice, because these colors affect the way we think and act. And, if we use color correctly in our public relations communications, we can affect the way our audiences react to our messages. The correct usage of color can help create moods that help establish our audiences' states of mind and influence their predilection to a specific behavior on our behalf. Whether used as backgrounds or in typefaces, color is a very powerful tool for establishing emotion. It can evoke similar reactions from most people.

Colors are basically warm, cool or neutral:

— Warm colors stimulate activity and creativity by eliciting a warm and exciting mood.

— Cool colors are passive and calming; they reduce tension and increase concentration.

— Neutral colors give a feeling of stability and balance.

Warm Colours

Red is the most emotionally intense color; it increases the metabolism, quickens the pulse, and stimulates breathing. Some of the words that describe its emotive effects are: Energy, passion, power, excitement, heat, danger, love, valor, hardiness, strength, blood, war, strength, sex, and speed. Red is generally less effective with men than it is with women, who prefer it over orange. Although red is the preferred "second color" in printed materials and on the web, use it cautiously (especially saturated reds). It is best used for thin borders but not for details.

Red clothes draw the attention of others, but they do make the wearer appear heavier. Red clothes are not helpful when negotiating. As far as food is concerned, it is very popular and elicits a good response from impulse buyers.

Orange is an autumn color with a strong personality and a declassifying, strong appeal. This color makes one feel happy, confident, creative, adventurous, playful, vibrant, and full of warmth. Men prefer it over red. It works best as a highlight tempered by heavy black detail. Interestingly, the color promotes hunger, and elicits good response from impulse buyers.

Yellow is the attention-getter that speeds metabolism. Interestingly it offers completely opposite emotive qualities. On the one hand, it evokes words such as: wisdom, playful, satisfying, optimistic, warmth, sunny day, cheer, optimism and happiness. Yet on the other hand, it indicates caution, decay, sickness and jealousy. It is less effective with women than with men. When used as type over a black background, it's the easiest to read. Yellow enhances concentration (that's why legal pads are yellow). But when used alone, it is the most difficult color for eyes to process.

Pink is the only warm color that has a tranquilizing effect. When one sees pink, one thinks of romance, of things soft and sweet, of security and nurturing. As such, it is used in bedrooms, and also by prisons to control violent inmates.

Cool Colours

Green is the color of nature, with calming, relaxing and

refreshing effects. It has these emotive qualities: Health, regeneration, contentment, harmony, life, growth, energy, faith, and money. Green connotes fertility in women, and masculinity, conservatism and wealth in men. It is used to create a sense of serenity. Be careful, different tones of green can do different things – for example, blue-green denotes class and restraints, but on the other hand, lime green doesn't work well in large areas. Green is easiest on the eyes, and is a popular food color.

Blue is the most popular color. It is proven to increase energy. Blue's emotive qualities are often described by these words: Honesty, integrity, trustworthiness, belonging, peaceful, tranquility, justice, vigilance, and perseverance. However, blue also connotes cold, coolness, depressing, solitude and sadness. It is less effective with women than it is with men. In web design and printed materials, avoid saturated blue, as it looks cheap, uncreative and amateurish. Ever wonder why text links are in blue? It's because they give better results (i.e., they draw more clicks than any other color). Bordering central areas of a webpage creates a sense of expansiveness. Blue elicits good response from budget buyers, but be careful, for it is the color of toxic foods.

Purple and Violet are symbolic of royalty. When one sees these colors, a person thinks of royalty, luxury, wealth, dignity, sophistication, and spirituality – or in a different vein, words such as feminine, romantic, mystic, beauty, and inspiration. Use them sparingly, because they are rare in nature and can appear artificial. They are also the color of toxic food.

Neutral Colours

Black is used almost exclusively for the printed word. Aside from its value in written communication, black connotes authority, power, formal, sophistication, elegance, seductiveness, and mystery. It is often associated with black magic, witches and demons, and the color implies submission and evil. Black clothes are stylish and timeless; they make people appear thinner, but can be overpowering. They make light-haired people appear to have inner strength and determination.

Gray is the color of executives. Take note of the walls in airports – they are usually dove gray, giving travelers a feeling of executives and business persons, or "high class." In printed and web materials, avoid dull grays, as they appear utilitarian. Light grayish-blue helps eliminate glare.

White is a summer color that reflects light. It symbolizes innocence, purity, chastity, virginity, youth, mildness, cleanliness and sterility. It goes with everything.

Brown is a good color for gathering more information as it encourages open conversation. The color symbolizes wood or leather; light brown symbolizes genuineness. Its emotive qualities are credibility and stability, and sometimes sadness or wistfulness. It's a popular food color.

Strategy vs Tactics

There is often confusion about the difference between a "strategy" and a "tactic." Occasionally, they are used interchangeably, and of course, this is a mistake.

Strategy involves the "big picture" – the overall plan, how the campaign will achieve organizational goals and objectives. It involves deciding who the important publics are and which of them will be the recipients of your messages (i.e., "target audiences"). Strategic planning helps determine how the organization will be positioned; it decides how important publics will learn about the organization and how it can help them. It will provide avenues of discovery to facilitate this. Strategic thinking will create a reason for the audience should believe and support the organization, and it will help develop a consistent message and focus for the organization to uphold.

Each strategy must be considered on its own merits, and must be a viable option to be judged on its own strengths – one that definitely will solve the problem. Any approaches that will not solve the problem independently should be eliminated. If a combination of approaches can solve the problem, consider the combination as a strategic alternative. Each alternative strategy should attain all audience objectives. All of the pros and cons of each strategy should be considered, and in the process, options are more easily identified.

Identifying business risks and opportunities creates the chance to exercise informed judgment. Viable options are vital – knowing each option's advantages and disadvantages will enable decision-making based on fact instead of emotion. Remember, you must take careful aim in everything you do in public relations. Don't shoot from the hip: you could end up with powder burns on your butt.

Tatics are activities specifically created and selected to reach specific and measurable objectives. Tactics are the actual ways in which the strategies are executed. They include newsletters, publicity, seminars, trade shows, advertising, Internet presence, and any other tool that target audiences actually are exposed to.

Tactics include:

— *Action events*: Non-written tactics such as special events, demonstrations, exhibits, parades, community contributions (manpower, talent, advice, money) and other non-verbal activities.

— *Communications tatics*: Verbal tactics (oral and written) that use words or pictures. These include newsletters, flyers, news releases, brochures, direct mail, advertising, themes, slogans, the World Wide Web (WWW), and other initiatives that use words and language as their basis.

In both action events and communications tactics, separate the initiatives into message tactics (which will be used to get your message directly to the audience), and media tactics (how the news media will be utilized to publicize action events).

Employee Relations

A company's employees are more than just a means to a profitable year. They mean more to an company than just a computer-generated page full of personnel expenses that can be juggled to meet quarterly goals as management sees fit. A business organization can be described in many ways; let's look at it in terms of human physiology. The following list is a little incomplete, but you get the idea:

— *Management serves as an organization's central nervous system*: It creates the intelligence, the strategy and the tactics, and communicates it throughout the organization.

— *Financial capital is the company's lifeblood*: It keeps things moving smoothly. It creates products that bring in nourishment to the organization and its various component parts.

— *Employees are its vital organs*: If there is nothing or no one to produce products and services, then the best ideas, the best strategies will wither and die in the organization.

Management, capital and employees. Which is the most important? All three are equally important. All three present unique challenges to an organization's success. Employees represent the largest and most important investment a company can make. Look at an company's list of expenses. Wages and salaries are right up there at the top. Therefore, doesn't it make sense that responsible management should do everything it can to nurture and protect its investment?

By virtue of their function, employees are a company's most important public. They are stakeholders in every sense of the word. The quality of their work, the depth of their commitment, the pride they hold for the company — these all earn them the right to know, and help determine, the destiny assigned to them by management. When a company needs to communicate, it should communicate first with its employees.

The public relations profession should participate in this two-way communication, this inter-relationship between management and employees. We have a responsibility to do so, because we have consciously — and with considerable forethought — accepted the roles of counselor, facilitator and mediator. We have laid claim to this turf, so we'd better put our money where our mouth is.

Public relations professionals lament about how human resources (HR) departments are stealing the work we have traditionally owned — they're in charge of training, they put out the employee newsletter, they arrange for orientation tours, they why, they do stuff that we should be doing.

Anybody can put out a newsletter, anybody can give a tour, anybody can arrange training. That's technician work. Technicians are a dime a dozen. You can build a stable of free-lance technicians as easily as you can hire competent young, entry-level public relations associates. Outsource the work if you have to. There's nothing wrong with technician work — we've all done it. It's just that each public relations professional should make it a personal goal to move beyond the technician level as soon as possible.

The profession should concern itself with the deeper questions: Why do we need to communicate? What is the ultimate behavior we expect our audiences to exhibit when we communicate with them? How can we tailor our delivery to ensure that the message is presented at a time when it will be most optimally accepted? We need to prove our value in employee relations strategy. The stakes are higher there. Responsible employee relations goes beyond the traditional suggestion boxes, newsletters, memoranda, exit interviews, work stoppages, and rewards and recognition.

To be sure, these aspects of employee relations are vital and should not be discarded. It's just that someone else can do some of this work — HR departments, freelancers — especially in these difficult times of downsizing and re-engineering. Companies cannot continue their traditional paternal existence. Maybe sometime in the future, but for now, times are tough. Earn a place in the management huddle. You can do more for your employees there than you can by writing about them in the employee newsletter or publicizing their promotions in the local newspaper.

4

Professional Responsibilities of Public Relations

Working as a counselor for a public relations agency gives a practitioner a sense of satisfaction when a job is done right. Know why? It has something to do with being outside the "immediate family" of a business, corporation or organization. A corporate public relations practitioner is part of the family. A community relations or public affairs director at a government agency or public utility is part of the family. Officers, secretaries, janitors, accountants — everyone who has a job in the organization — is part of the family. Agency people, on the other hand, are not. We're — well, we're more like adopted children.

That's not necessarily bad. As outsiders, we have a different point of view. We're not so caught up in the day-to-day routine that we can't spot subtle communications problems hiding right under our noses. In fact, being an outsider is one of the things that makes us valuable. Agency satisfaction has something to do with personal achievement, or a sense of worth. Perhaps, even a little bit of egotism. But in the public relations profession, achievement, worth and egotism are not unique to agency practitioners.

The overriding reason why it's satisfying to work for an agency is the fact that as outsiders, we are entrusted by clients with their time and money. Our clients commit their good reputation to our hands, and give us access to business secrets, their hard-earned money, and personnel hours. And, as responsible professionals, we take that trust and use it to accomplish something good.

A good analogy is the trust the American people had (and still have) in our nuclear defense system. Despite criticism and protest, the fact remains that a great many Americans see a need for nuclear defense — particularly the ominous Minutemen missiles that sat in silos throughout North America. Whether or not we as individuals agree that they should have been there, or that fellow Americans should have been asked to send them skyward when appropriate signals are received, we had to trust that those responsible for their operation knew what they were doing. Even the detractors had to trust them.

We have to trust that they will do the right thing at the right time. We have to trust that the system on supports correct decisions and will not allow a mistake. We have to trust that the buttons will not be pushed by a madman. Similarly, our clients trust us. And let's face it — client trust has to be earned, and justified, every single day. So it is our professional responsibility not to betray that trust. As agency public relations counselors, we often hold the success or failure of a project, campaign — or maybe even the business itsellf — in our hands. Unless we become "The Good Hands People," we'll lose that precious client trust. Once it's lost, it will never be recovered. Reputations can tumble with amazing alacrity — bad news indeed does travel fast.

Good work stays with us a long time. Bad work stays with us forever. Our clients trust us. So, we have to justify — we have to earn — that trust. How? What are the professional responsibilities we need to fulfill?

Apublic relations counselor should be four things: A counselor should be honest and candid, a counselor should pay attention to details, a counselor should be creative, and a counselor should be a team member.

If we are nothing else, we must be honest and open with clients. Nothing will destroy a counselor-client relationship faster than a lie or a hidden truth. Just as we have a right to expect forthright information from our clients, so your clients have a right to our frank and honest counsel. As counselors, we must resist every temptation to talk our way out of our clients' tough, probing questions. If we don't know the answer to a question, we should say so. We should promise to have the answer at the earliest possible moment, and we should follow through diligently on that promise.

We cannot lie to the publics with whom we're trying to communicate. We cannot lie to the media. We cannot lie to ourselves. And most of all, we cannot lie to our clients. Public relations counselors must be ethical, and must uphold the highest business standards. After all, we represent our clients in public, and serve as a bridge between them and the news media, between them and the general public. That's why the ethics codes are so important.

The Public Relations Society of America's Code of Professional Standards for the Practice of Public Relations — its Code of Ethics — for example, is like the Constitution of the United States of America — it's the guiding light of the organization, it defines the rights and ground rules for its members, it lays a foundation for honest and frank dialogue, and it's a living document that changes with the times. Honesty and candor in public relations counseling also means that you will not accept a client whose goals and objectives are not consistent with your own ethical and moral standards. We cannot be expected to do our best work for a client we don't respect.

Agencies often take on clients and campaigns knowing full well that only a partial success can be expected. And this is okay, if the challenge is there, and if the campaign's goals and objectives address the possibility of failure. What is not okay is when we do so solely for the fees the job will bring. We should turn down clients and jobs that require us to compromise our standards. And when we turn down a client, we should tell them why. That's the hardest part, of course. It's easy to say yes, it's hard to say no. And for most of us, it's even harder to explain why we have to say no. But we have to do it. It's part of being responsible.

Being Responsible in Details

Being a responsible professional means taking care of details — even the seemingly insignificant ones. Every fact should be double-checked. Every piece of communication should be verified by the client. Every news release, every paragraph, every word should be checked for spelling and grammatical errors. We are word merchants. The words we send out reflect on our professionalism, and they reflect even more so on the clients for whom we've submitted them.

As counselors, we must create a checklist for every project and event. We must make sure we've seen to every little detail, and prepared for every contingency. We all hold brainstorming sessions in the course of our creative work. Why not set aside a portion of every brainstorming session for some "negative brainstorming"? It works this way: Think up every reason why the campaign will fail. What if it rains? What if the CEO becomes ill the day he's supposed to conduct a press conference? What if there's an accident? What if the announcements come back for additional postage on the day of the event? What if a key logistics person is stalled in traffic? Then, work up a contingency solution to each problem.

It's only possible to think up logical solutions to problems that are identified. If they crop up at crucial points along the way, problems will wreak havoc on any well-intentioned communications plan. Like Boy Scouts, we have to be prepared. We have to pay attention to details. If we don't do it, who will? The client? Our clients trust us to handle the details, advise them of potential problems and recommended solutions, and guide their course of action.

Assuming that all public relations counselors are equally competent and professionally responsible, what makes one stand out in the crowd? It's creativity. It's the ideas that keep our profession growing. It's establishing new and creative channels of communication that makes our work exciting. Any public relations counselor worth his salt can rattle off at least a dozen ways to communicate with any given public — newsletters, press releases, brochures, e-mail, advertising, plant tours, exhibits, special mailings, educational videos, speakers bureaus, radio public service announcements, press conferences, the Worldwide Web, scholarships, and community relations projects are some of the tools we use.

But aside from the tried and true, the memorable events are the ones that emerge from brainstorming sessions. Creative brainstorming is the way great communication is created. Brainstorming works on the theory that 1 + 1 = 3. In other words, the sum of the parts is greater than the whole. Two people working together can do more than two people working on their own. It's called"synergy." We owe it to our clients to be as creative as we can be. Every effort should be made to channel our mental energies toward our clients' benefit.

If 1 + 1 = 3, then it stands to reason that a team (1 + 1 + 1 + 1 + 1, ad infinitum) can change the world. A team made up of the client, the counselor, other agency personnel, graphic designers and other creative people can do more than a counselor working alone can do. Counselors have to love public relations work enough to let some of it go, in the best interest of the client. Keeping a project close to the vest simply because we want total control does our clients a disservice. We in fact deprive the client of the one valuable commodity that sets us apart from our competitors — our creativity.

A one-person show can be effective, and it does have advantages, not the least of which is total control. Unfortunately, some practitioners have a need, or a desire, to be indispensable. That's too bad, for ultimately, no one is indispensable. To be sure, being a one-person show has its disadvantages as well — lack of team back-up, for one. If a counselor is ill, or out of town, or simply tied up on another project, and if you have no one to call on for back-up, the client will suffer. Not good. The client pays our bills. We cannot operate alone, or in secrecy.

Counselors working alone in secrecy are not fulfilling their responsibilty to the client. Being a responsible professional also means we all do our share (and more) of the work assigned to us as a team member. The team is only as strong — as creative, as effective — as its so-called "weakest" member. Fulfill the minimum requirements, the job will get done. Exceed the minimum requirements, and it shows in superior results — the project is successful beyond expectations, and the communications impact is consumate.

What it all boils down to is this. If we accept professional responsibility, if we are honest and forthright, and if we possess all the aforementioned qualities of a responsible public relations professional, then we will be successful counselors. More importantly, we will be friends and valuable business assets to our clients.

Public Relations Programmes: A Divergent Phenomena

All sound public relations programs, campaigns, and decisions are the combined result of three similar, yet widely divergent phenomena – highways, tributaries, and bunny trails. Each is a path from here to there, yet each has its own elemental uniqueness that, when taken in toto with the other two, helps form the basis of lucid strategy and tactical selection.

Highways provide the straight and narrow – the most logical and efficient way of getting from point A to point B. The thoroughfare is well-paved and well-engineered, the route is tested and proven, and the guidelines are historic and easy to follow. There are signs to guide the way, there are rest stops and roadside points of interest, and they are plotted on maps. Tributaries are feeders that originate at sources far from the main river. They pick up material along the way and add them to the stream. Tributaries contribute to the efficacy and power of the flow, and what they bring in volume and material will help determine the potency, and often the direction, of the onrush. They are directly responsible for growth. They too are plotted on maps (up to a point, for the smaller ones are usually ignored).

Bunny trails are close to being the antitheses of the orderly progression established by highways and tributaries. They cause our forward progress to head off in different directions. You know how bunnies are; they constantly make right-angle turns, poking their noses here and there, often reversing their direction. Whether foraging or fleeing, they make it difficult to predict where they are heading next. And yet, they always seem to make it back to the warren (their point B) safely. Like highways, every decision that we make starts out at the beginning – with basic research, careful thought, and the setting of goals and objectives. "We are here, and this is where we want to go." We know the direction, the difficulties ahead, and how much time and resources are required. We can gauge our speed, and we know what and who we have to pick up along the way. Our basic course, our movement from point A to point B, is set.

But we don't live in a vacuum. Our plans can never be concrete because we don't know everything there is to know. We require the assistance of tributaries. From all sides comes a flow of new information and resources that we can use to make our journey more efficient in the long run. Some of these tributaries move into our sphere of influence through our own efforts – it is vital to initiate inquiries that pay off in strategic data and the delivery of funding for our campaign. Other tributaries just happen; they find us and enrich us with unexpected help.

Still, a juggernaut that ignores what else is "out there" can be efficient, yet ineffective. That's where the bunny trails become important role-players in our decision-making. Planned bunny trails, that is. Occasionally, we need to wander – to move off the straight and narrow, to wander away from the beaten path. We need to explore the wilderness and to breathe the fresh air. We need to examine the flowers and the people who live out of the mainstream. We need to measure what will elicit the behavior that will define our campaign, and whether or not new direction is indicated. So we take the side roads and trust to serendipity.

If we work this right, our decision making will be enriched by contributions both solicited and unsolicited. If we keep our eyes and ears open – if we truly see and listen – then our arrival at point B will have more meaning. It will affect more people positively, and it will facilitate more-than-satisfactory end results.

Why the Public Doesn't Understand Public Relations

Ask anybody you know — business leaders included — about their impression of public relations. Or, they will look at you for a second or two, scrunch up their eyebrows, attempt to mumble something, then completely give up. Then, what if they ask you the same question? Very few practitioners can answer in plain and simple language, very few can define public relations in 15 words or less without describing the tactical things that we do.

As public relations practitioners, we've all had to live through what others have said about us. At times, it sure does rankle to have our profession maligned. Do any of these sound familiar?

— They're SPIN DOCTORS! Born in the political arena and perpetuated by television, "spin doctoring" is employed by spokespersons who try to manipulate an issue (and their adversaries' responses) to their own advantage.

- It's just a PR PLOY! The attempt to influence public opinion is often thought of as being synonymous with "tricks," with "lying" and with "manipulation." And the perception is that we do this to fool people into doing what we want them to do.
- It's only ORGANIZED LYING! The public often perceives that communications initiatives are planned with one end in mind – to fool people.
- PR is FREE ADVERTISING! You hear this a lot. The public accuses public relations of being too cheap to pay for ads, and of manipulating the news media to run stories with a slanted point of view that benefits only a few people.
- They're MANIPULATORS who know how to STRETCH THE TRUTH! Because public relations advocates and persuades, the profession is often accused of manipulating and using people and the news media to the client's/company's advantage, preying on the public's good intentions.
- EXAGGERATION & HYPERBOLE! The truth is stretched, we overstate, we over-promise – "Biggest! Best!" "You can't afford NOT to vote 'Yes' on the proposition!"

Maybe the public have a basis for criticism. Let's look at some reasons why:

- Public relations has its roots in propaganda. "Propaganda" has turned into a dirty word that describes despicable attempts to couch the truth, to persuade the public to a certain point of view, and often to deliberately create an "enemy" that must be overcome at all costs. In actuality, the word means "propagate," to plant and nurture good things, and was used extensively by the Catholic Church to spread the word of their religion.

— The news media takes potshots at us all the time. They paint a nasty picture of our work. They ignore accomplishments of public relations professionals, not reporting them in their newspapers or on the air. Their audiences pick this up, and they react accordingly.

— We often do shoddy work. And that's unacceptable. It doesn't help when the public views the results of poorly conceived public relations initiatives. It doesn't help when our only visible work is the occasional (albeit often creative) PR stunts that are entertaining, but seem unfocused and frivolous.

— We support unpopular causes – abortion, pornography, smokers' rights – for whatever reason: the money, or for reasons related personal freedom. Everybody deserves an advocate, and we often are willing to provide our services. Our clients often are controversial – the Church of Scientology, the National Rifle Association, tobacco companies, alcohol companies, unpopular governments, despots and tyrants.

d— Anybody can do publicity. Let's face it. Professionalism aside, anybody can write a few facts on their event, take it to a reporter, answer questions, and see their story printed somewhere, or broadcast somewhere. It's not hard. What makes the difference is professionalism and persuasion, requisites when asking someone to pay for work. But, accept the fact that anybody can do publicity. No wonder the public doesn't respect us for that.

— We ask inexperienced practitioners to bite off more than they can chew. You do not become a professional by being paid for doing something. You become a professional through education, experience and recognition by your peers as someone they'd call on in a pinch.

— Sometimes, we don't train our entry-level practitioners adequately before throwing them to the wolves. They're expected to hit the ground running. True professionals would not allow this to happen. Instead, they would teach, nurture and mentor those with promise.

— We ignore the research much of the time. Even worst, we do no research at all. Or, we have not focused in tightly on what our goals and objectives should be, and consequently, cannot measure our results.

— Finally, we let them do it. How many times have you seen an aspersion that rankles you, and said, "Someone should correct this," then swallow hard and not fight back.

Societal changes have something to do with the way we're viewed. People seem to be a lot ruder and inconsiderate these day. Examples abound: At a recent Public Relations Society of America national conference, a video address by U.S. House Speaker Newt Gingrich was booed down; people are shooting each other on our freeways; national news magazines write cover stories on the new intolerance. Watergate probably has something to do with this. People no longer trust government. The news media has become more cynical and intrusive. The national psyche underwent a traumatic transformation during the congressional hearings.

We are all under tremendous social pressure to succeed in an era of reengineering and downsizing, having to do more for less, being required to prove their worth, wanting to keep up with the Joneses, wanting bigger homes and nicer cars — money, money, money! We worry about our health and safety. The era of sexual freedom came crashing down with the rise of herpes, young people now have to worry about HIV and AIDS, older people are fearful of Alzheimer's disease, cancer is more prevalent, automobile accidents and airline crashes seem to occur more frequently, and there is always the specter of a DUI incident every time we get into a car.

Society is more litigious. The number of product liability suits is going through the roof. Frivolous suits are filed every day by unreasonable people who are "gonna get mine before someone else does." Are lawyers to blame for this misunderstanding? More and more, lawyers are practicing public relations on the courthouse steps, "spinning" their own version of what's happening in the courtroom. And they're not afraid to lie and manipulate either.

At the 1993 conference of the Association for Educators in Journalism and Mass Communication, attorney Eric Naiburg (legal counsel for the infamous Amy Fisher) admitted making up stories and lying to the news media. People see this, and they call it PR. People see this, and they blame us. Could it be the news media's fault? The news media and public relations engage in a self-proclaimed "love/hate relationship." They assume that public relations diverts attention from the truth, equivocates, deflects and misdirects.

The pretenders — the charlatans who pose as professionals — must share some of the blame. After all, they have no training, and are doing our work poorly. And then there are the corporations — close-mouthed, anti-media, so untrusting that they'd rather stonewall the media, stonewall the activists who are "in their face," and oftentimes, even stonewall the local community.

The first questions we need to ask in anything we do in public relations are: "Is there really a problem to fix?" and "Does anybody care?" Well, somebody does care — those who are trying to make the public relations profession great, those who believe our counsel is indispensable, those who are proud of the work we do. The profession's future effectiveness and existence depends on its practitioners caring about why the public doesn't understand what we do. The vast majority of our colleagues is ethical and competent. We have a tremendous source of knowledge, influence, power and collegiality that if focused, can make this point.

Public relations provides a natural atmosphere for business partnering, arbitration and negotiation. And, we have an obligation to the public good because of the power we wield. We work from the inside, complementing the work that the good-intentioned news media attempts to accomplish from the outside. We have the ability to influence policy that will benefit society. We work better from the inside. Why should we care? Because it's the right thing to do. Let's face it. It's our own damned fault that the public doesn't understand what we do. And we should care. So, what can we do? Here's a starter list:

— Stop distributing misleading information.

— Wield our power judiciously.

— Forget hyperbole and exaggeration.

— Practice candor and forthrightness.

— Get involved in policy decisions.

— Be willing to be held accountable.

— Contribute to the bottom line.

— Put our jobs on the line.

— Eliminate conflicts of interest, remove ourselves from decisions if necessary.

— Don't give in to temptations of money, influence and/or power.

— Keep our values intact.

— Increase our personal credibility.

— Do our work with the public interest in mind.

— Don't over-promise.

— Work to beef up codes of ethics, abide by them.

— Serve the " Five Masters" well — self, client, employer, profession, and society.

Why doesn't the public understand public relations? Because we haven't given them a good reason to, that's why.

RULES OF PUBLIC RELATIONS PROFESSIONALS

Miyamoto Musashi was a noted 17th-Century Japanese samurai, who in 1643 established a number of "rules" to be followed in learning the art of military sciences, focusing on war as a purely pragmatic enterprise. He paid particular attention to psychology and physics, all of which centered on victory as the essence of warfare. In 1643, Miyamoto put his thoughts together in *The Book of Five Rings*. It has been translated by Thomas Cleary, Ph.D., a professor of East Asian Languages and Civilizations at Harvard University, and was published by Shambhala in 1993.

Miyamoto presented nine rules for learning the art of military science that are remarkable in their foresight, and they have been used by business strategists over the years to attain and maintain tactical and strategic advantage in the business "battleground." Although the balance (and bulk) of Miyamoto's treatise deals with specific tactics on both offensive and defensive uses of weaponry and strategy, these nine principles nicely serve as a cornerstone for the practice of public relations. Specific mind-sets and techniques for moves and counter-moves can easily be related to, and applied to the work public relations professionals encounter daily.

But for the purposes of this treatment, let's just concentrate on these nine preliminary principles. Miyamoto's nine rules of "The Art" are: Think of what is right and true, practice and cultivate the science, become acquainted with the arts, know the principles of the crafts, understand the harm and benefit in everything, learn to see everything accurately, become aware of what is not obvious, be careful even in small matters, and do not do anything useless.

Think of What is Right and True

As public relations professionals, do what is best in the public interest. Just as warfare should be utilized to support benevolent ends (*e.g.*, to eliminate tyranny and provide freedom for the oppressed), so should public relations have a loftier goal to serve the public good. The strategies and actions that are selected must in the end provide results that are best for your company or organization. And at the very end, your decisions should move toward doing what is best for you personally, for you are the one who must sleep at night knowing the consequences of your actions.

Practice and Cultivate the Science

In public relations, as in warfare, we have a wealth of past experience to fall back upon. We know things that work, and things that don't work. We need to study the success and failures of the past so we can increase our own chances. It is extremely important that we learn from what others have worked hard to prove, and that we don't waste our time and the resources of our organization. Study what has and has not worked before. In other words, do exhaustive research, then do more research. And when you're done, research some more.

Part of the academic process is the sharing of information with others. Unfortunately, business professionals hold strategies very close to the vest, to maintain their competitive advantage. Business secrets, after all, are business secrets. However, remember that two very important phenomena result from sharing: First, everybody benefits with the shared knowledge, the quality of our work improves, and the profession progresses. Second, the standards are raised. The knowledge base increases, and what you once learned in your fifth year as a public relations professional is now required entry-level knowledge.

Become Acquainted With the Arts

Miyamoto advises studying the arts — he of course was referring not only to the martial arts, but the fine arts and the work of craftsmen and artisans (who are discussed in

Rule 4) as well. Essentially, what he was talking about was using talents and creativity to the best of one's ability. The mind is a powerful thing. The sheer power of thought can accomplish so much in itself, before a finger is lifted to accomplish any task.

Anything a person's mind can conceive and believe, can most certainly be achieved — even the most impossible of challenges can be surmounted if one's thoughts are channeled to the hands of the artisan. Artists have much to teach us — patience, excellence, making the right choices, study and research, conservation of motion and energy, making all the parts fit, thinking things out before making the master stroke, examining options, expanding the mind.

Know the Principles of the Crafts

There are certain qualities to be learned from craftsmen. The precise nature of their work demands constant and focused attention to technique and detail. Craftsmen work with their hands, just as many public relations practitioners work with their hands. In either case, those plying their trade become artists in their own right, creating objects of functional beauty in the case of craftsmen, and works of advocacy that can influence a generation in the case of public relations. It is important therefore to know one's limitations, and when the need arises, to call upon the talents of others. For we are not super-people.

Rather, we have a unique ability to think and reason, and when this power is shared with others, something very special occurs — synergy. The whole is greater than the sum of the parts. Craftsmen and artisans are experts in what they do. Public relations practitioners also become experts in what they do, but it behooves them to become more. The sharing of ideas and techniques, successes and failures, will serve to expand the body of knowledge that will become the basis and frame of reference for those who would be our legacies.

Understand the Harm and Benefit in Everything

"Win-win" is an over-used phrase. Still, it's something we should all strive for. However, that in any campaign that requires people to choose sides, there are those who are going to be hurt. The goal therefore, is to win, while inflicting the least amount of damage to those whom you must later convert. Everything that's done in war or in public relations has consequences. The very nature of our work is advocacy — we are part of that army of "special pleaders," who serve as spokespeople for our companies, our organizations, our causes. Without conflict, there would be no need for the public relations profession.

In the end, the needs of the many will outweigh the needs of the few (or the one) — this, from of all things, a movie — a quote by Leonard Nimoy's character "Spock" in *Star Trek II: The Wrath of Kahn*. Essentially, what must remembered is that in our society, we favor the majority, with sensitivity toward the rights of the minorities. Thus, know that there is harm — as well as benefit — in everything that we do.

Learn to See Everything Accurately

It is important to visualize your success. It's that "Vision Thing" that President George Bush kept referring to. It's what Maxwell Maltz called "psychocybernetics" in the '70s. It's what the Rev. Norman Vincent Peale was talking about when he coined the phrase, "The Power of Positive Thinking." This vision is important. If you can see your success, you will succeed. If you see failure, then you will fail. The warrior must go into battle knowing that victory is his for the taking. Public relations professions must go into campaigns convinced that their counsel is sound, that the tactics we have selected will attain the objectives and goals that we have set.

Still, temper your enthusiasm and optimism with a healthy dose of reality. In warfare and public relations, there is no place for rose-colored glasses. There is simply too much at stake. In war, it's casualties and causes. In public relations, it's jobs, it's causes, it's the very existence of our companies and organizations. There is no room for shooting from the hip. Don't trust your eyes. Ask for help. Hire the best people, the best visionaries.

Become Aware of What is Not Obvious

Look for hidden problems. Remember that nothing is as it seems on the surface. Trees that resembled a forest moving in the wind proved to be the downfall of Macbeth. A wooden horse mistaken as a gift of capitulation proved to be the downfall of the Spartans. A few dissidents who opposed an oppressive rule hid behind a seemingly tranquil populace to overthrow a king and found a new nation. A misreading of public sentiment sent Coca Cola reeling and retreating when it introduced New Coke. Nothing is ever as it seems. You have to ask lots of questions. You have to ask these questions of the right people.

Be Careful Even in Small Matters

The success of a battle, of a war, of a cause, is in the details. The success of a public relations project, of a campaign, of a cause, is also in the details. Everything counts. The smallest *faux pas* — the most seemingly insignificant miscalculation — will be your downfall.

Do Not do Anything Useless

First question to ask before entering a war: "Why are we fighting?" First question to ask before starting a public relations campaign: "Is there a problem?" Focus on the problem and eliminate everything that (although attractive and flashy and attention-getting) is unnecessary. Do this right at the start, before you get deep into your planning. As public relations professionals, we must know what needs to be done, what we want to accomplish with our efforts. This is behavioral public relations, pure and simple. What exactly do you want your target audience to do when you've communicated with them?

As with any military campaign, a public relations campaign must set well-thought-out, well-defined, easily measured, very specific objectives – many small accomplishments that when taken as a whole, result in success.

Other thoughts as they apply to public relations are;

— You can hardly become a master of martial arts (public relations) unless you see the immediate in a broad context.

— Keep martial arts (public relations) on your mind, and work diligently in a straightforward manner.

— You can overcome people (problems) by means of your body (knowledge and ability).

— Large-scale military science (public relations) is a matter of winning at keeping good people, winning at taking care of the populace, winning at carrying out customary social observances.

— When you reach this point, how could you be defeated?

Comprehensive Public Relations Plan

The public relations plan is one of the most important documents you will produce in your career. It has been said that public relations is the result of form and substance. While this is not exactly true, it does have some basis when you're trying to persuade your client or boss to let you spend their money. How you say it (form) and what you say (substance) will likely determine your success or failure in getting your proposal accepted.

Let's face it, clients and bosses are impressed by the way things look — just like you, they're only human. All other things being equal, a well-organized and attractively prepared proposal will win out every time. So, what can you do to help ensure success? Well, there are a number of elements in an effective public relations proposal presentation of which you must be aware.

Letter of Transmittal

This item is an adjunct to — and precedes — the actual plan. As simple as it may sound, you need to transmit your plan to the client or your boss. Standard accepted business practice dictates that you write a letter or memorandum of transmittal. Limit the transmittal letter/memo to a single page. If you are submitting the plan to a client, use the following format:

— A cordial opening paragraph stating that you are submitting "the attached plan for XXX campaign, as promised." Follow this with a brief description of the plan, including the campaign's "bottom line" — income expectations, expenses, net "profit" or loss — in other words, what your client is expected to lay out for the public relations campaign.

— A reference to the executive summary that follows.

— A statement that you either look forward to presenting the plan in person as a previously designated time and place, or will contact the client to arrange a meeting to discuss the plan.

— Gracious words of "thank you" for the opportunity to submit the plan.

Executive Summary

Also an adjunct to the plan, this is a summary of your proposed campaign that covers several key points most likely to interest the executive who reads your plan. Here is a suggested format:

— The Problem: State here what you believe the problem to be.

— Program Goal: State here what your ultimate goal is.

— Target Audiences: (1) Your primary audience, (2) your secondary (intervening) audience(s), and (3) your tertiary (special) audience(s).

— Audience Objectives: (1) What you expect your primary audience to do, (2) what you expect your intervening audience(s) to do, and (3) what you expect your special audience(s) to do.

— Major Strategy: State your major strategy here, listing the key tactics that you will use in your campaign.

— Recommended Budget: State your total anticipated income and sources, your anticipated expenses, and the anticipated net profit or loss.

— Evaluation Plans: State how you expect to evaluate (and expect to know) whether or not you've achieved each of your campaign and audience objectives.

Situation Analysis

The very first item in the plan itself should be an analysis of the current situation, based on results of your research. The situation analysis contains all of the information and data you collected about the internal and external environments. Depending on how much research is required and has been conducted, and how complicated and/or involved the organization's problems are, the situation analysis can run from one to three or more pages.

While a problem statement directs the planning effort to a particular set of conditions, the situation analysis provides details about internal and external contexts. It includes a literature review (which requires a bibliography of sources).

Internal Factors

— Statements of the organization's mission, charter, bylaws, history and structure.

— Lists, biographical sketches and photos of key individuals —officers, board members, and program managers.

— Detailed descriptions of programs, products, services, etc.

— Statistics about resources, budget, staffing and programs.

— Summaries of interviews with key personnel about the problem situation.

— Copies of policy statements and procedures related to the problem.

— Complete descriptions of how the organization currently handles the problem.

— Lists and descriptions of the organization's controlled communication media.

External Factors

— Clippings from newspapers, magazines, trade publications, and newsletters tracing print media coverage of organization and problem situation.

— Reports of radio, television and cable placements.

— Content analyses of media coverage.

— Lists of media, journalists, columnists, and free-lance writers who report news about the organization and related issues.

— Lists and descriptions of individuals and groups that share the organization's concerns, interests, and views (including their controlled print and broadcast media).

— Lists and descriptions of individuals and groups that oppose the organization's positions on the issues (including their controlled print and broadcast media).

— Survey results of public's awareness, knowledge, opinions, and behaviors related to the organization and problem situation.

— Schedules of special events, observances, and other important dates related to the organization and problem.

— Lists of government agencies, legislators, and officials with regulatory or legislative power affecting the organization and the problem situation.

— Copies of relevant government regulations, legislation, bills pending, referenda, publications, and hearing reports.

— Copies of published research on topics related to the problem situation.

— Lists of important reference books, records, and directories, as well as their locations in the organization.

When you write the situation analysis, present your research findings in a logical and easily understood order. List results of client research, situational research, and audience research. If you have used the suggested outline above, you should have all of the necessary pertinent information you need.

No matter how much research you've done, something always seems to be missing. If you've done your homework well, you should have no assumptions to present here. In some cases, however, assumptions are inevitable and as a practical matter, unavoidable. So, when you write your situation analysis, you may need to make some assumptions about various aspects of the situation. If you must make assumptions, list them in a supplemental section, noting what missing information you can reasonably assume. "A friendly media" is not a valid assumption. Professionals never make assumptions, especially about the news media.

Problems and Consequences

Based on your research, and particularly on your preliminary interviews with the client, you should be able to isolate the overriding problem, and determine what will happen if the problem is not solved. The problem statement itself should be concise and very specific. If possible, write it in 25 words or less, using standard subject-verb-object order. This step is crucial to your plan and to the success of your campaign. Mess up here and you will end up 'way off course. Think of the problem statement as your starting course to the moon. One degree to the left or right, up or down, and you'll miss the moon by thousands of miles.

It's the same with the problem statement. Identify the wrong problems, and you may as well not even turn in your plan. Get to the root cause of your problem, and try to identify exactly what attitude (what they think) or behavior (what they do) you need to influence. Do you want attitudes crystallized, modified or reinforced? Be especially conscious of the ultimate behavior you want to evoke. And yet, proper problem identification and statement is still not enough. The client may recognize that there is a problem, but unless there is a consequence —- unless the client will lose something of value, whether it be profits, members, or quality of service — the client may remain unconvinced about your plan. You must show the client what could result if something isn't done to correct the problem identified above. Explain in one concise declarative sentence what the consequences will be.

Goals are general directions, somewhat nebulous, that are not specific enough to be measured. Think of the word "go." It has no end. A good example is the signature line of the *Star Trek* television series: "To boldly go where no man ("no one" in *Generations*) has gone before." You can't measure it, and you probably will never know if the goals were accomplished, because once humans have gone somewhere, we've been there, and there are still other places to go since the universe is infinite and has no end. Objectives, on the other hand, are specific and measurable. They can be output objectives, or they can be attitudinal or behavioral. But most of all, they can be measured. They are concise. They are specific. Think of the word "object." You can touch it, it's there, it's actual, it's finite.

Audience Identification

Audience identification is vital to your campaign. You need to talk to the right people. You need to conserve valuable funds, time and manpower, and you cannot do this unless you target your publics carefully. A word about publics, stakeholders and audiences: A "public" is a group of people with similar interests. "Stakeholders" are a special kind of public, composed of people who have a particular interest (or "stake") in your organization. An "audience" is a public with whom you are communicating.

You need to find some intelligent answers to some equally intelligent questions.

— Who exactly is going to be affected by your public relations campaign? Who exactly are you trying to persuade?

— You're going to need some cooperation from others; who will this be? Where are these people located? How can you find them? How can you get in touch with them?

— The people you want to reach listen to opinion leaders; exactly who are these opinion leaders? Who and where are those credible, authoritative sources that your intended audience believes, and who can help you get your messages across?

— Your audiences generally act the way you do — they do the same things you do. What magazines and newspapers do they read? What radio stations do they tune in to? What TV shows do they watch? To what clubs and organizations do they belong? What professional associations do they join? What are their favorite charities? What are their children's favorite participation sports?

Generally speaking, there are three types of audiences:

Primary: This is the audience or public that you specifically want to influence. It's the people whose behavior you're trying to change. Influence them, and you've done your job well.

Secondary: These are "intervening" audiences. These are people who can intervene on your behalf and influence the primary audience. Convince them that you're right, and they can help you get to the primary audience. You've heard of "third-party testimonials" that are more credible than your direct communication? Secondary audiences are those "third-party" people. Influence the secondary audiences and your job will become a bit easier. Their "endorsement" of your cause serves as their "testimonial."

Teritary: These are "special" publics composed primarily of organized groups (e.g., clubs, councils, associations) that can mobilize quickly and endorse your cause. They usually have an established means of communication with their membership via newsletters and other media.

In your plan, identify who these people are, then prioritize them. Like the "inverted-pyramid" style of journalistic writing, audience prioritization will allow you to eliminate potential audiences from the bottom-up should the need arise because of budget cuts, time constraints or manpower reductions. Once you've identified and prioritized your audiences in your plan, tell the client exactly what message you believe should be directed to each of the audiences you have selected.

Like the problem statement, your messages should be direct and declaratory, and they should articulate specific benefits to the audiences. Try out a number of messages, then settle on one per audience, selecting the one you consider most important to your campaign goal.

Audience Objectives

In general, there must be at least one objective per audience. This is usually sufficient. In come cases, however, you will have more than one objective for each audience. Objectives should measure impact. Behavioral objectives are preferred, but the objectives can also be attitudinal, or informational. Objectives also can measure your output — what you did. But unless output is central to your problem and contributes to solutions, try to keep these to a minimum.

State your objectives in specific and quantifiable (measurable) terms whenever possible. Set them in a time frame, and if you know what the budget is, tell the client what you expect the cost to be. The objectives should be reachable, they should be acceptable to the client, and they must be ethical. A crystal-clear objective would read something like this: "Our objective is to deliver X results by Y date at a cost of Z dollars." Think of the goals as the treasure at the top of a stairway, and the objectives as the stairs.

Strategies

In this section, you need to present a number of strategies, each of which will in itself solve the problem. This is one of the hardest sections to complete, especially for inexperienced practitioners who must rely on information provided by others, rather than on personal experience. However, it is so essential to the campaign's success that every effort must be made to present excellent strategic alternatives. There are four basic strategies:

— Do nothing (inactive).

— Do something only if necessary (reactive).

— Do something before a problem arises (proactive).

— Involve others in solving or heading off problems (interactive).

It may also be feasible to take a "multi-active" approach to solving the problem, in which case you would use elements from each basic type of strategy. Whatever strategy is finally selected, know that it will help determine the success or failure of your proposed program. You may find it easier to select a strategy after reviewing the list of public relations initiatives (tactics, activities) that you will develop after conducting a number of creative brainstorming sessions.

Do not — repeat, do not — use the terms "inactive,""reactive," "proactive," "interactive," or "multi-active" in your plan, unless the client fully understands the terms and initiates their usage. The words can be considered public relations jargon and often are meaningless to the client. Don't use these words as crutches in an attempt to avoid explaining your strategy in detail.

State that each strategy, when considered on its own merits independently of the other alternative strategies, is a viable option to be judged on its own strengths, and will definitely solve the problem. Eliminate any approach you believe will not solve the problem on its own. If a combination of approaches can solve the problem, list the combination as a strategic alternative.

Each alternative strategy will attain all of the objectives listed earlier. Again, each individual solution must be feasible, appropriate and acceptable. All possible solutions should be considered and presented — unless, of course, your particular problem is one of those rare cases that has but a single solution. No, strike that notion. Don't be tempted by this intriguing possibility. Assume that your problem has two or more solutions.

Discuss all of the pros and cons of each strategy considered. In doing so, try to offer options to the client. If you can identify business risks and opportunities, you give the client an opportunity to exercise informed judgement. Clients need viable options — they need to know each option's advantages and disadvantages — in order to make decisions based on fact instead of emotion.

Clients don't want to "shoot from the hip." They want to make rational decisions. Remember, you must take careful aim in everything you do in public relations. Don't shoot from the hip: you could end up with powder burns on your butt. Finally, tell the client what your recommended approach or strategy is. Be sure to tell the client why you recommend this particular strategy, and be prepared to defend your choice under withering fire and challenge from the client. You can't fake this part. It may be helpful to refer to the pros and cons you listed for each strategic alternative.

Integrated Communication

Several issues arise when the term "integrated communications" is used. In this section only three of them will be described. (1) the abortive attempt by the marketing discipline to usurp both the advertising and public relations functions, (2) what integrated communications can do for the client, and (3) what integrated communications cannot do.

Marketing's Usurpation Ploy

Most of the marketing people have the arrogant attitude that marketing drives everything in the business world. And to an extent, their arguments hold water. After all, marketing controls communications in so many ways, from the creation of a product and/or service, to the moment that it is consumed or used by the customer. No argument there. In the so-called "marketing mix" — a "flavor-of-the-month" term used in the '70s — marketing takes the lead. Advertising delivers the specific message to the ultimate consumer via paid messages; public relations can deliver additional customer awareness through promotional activities and publicity. Advertising and public relations play supportive roles in product/service awareness.

Role of IC

What IC can do

Integrated communications makes total sense. If you were going to attempt to influence a potential buyer to purchase and use your product, wouldn't you use every means of persuasive communications at your disposal to influence the purchasing decision? Of course, you would. You would use product design, packaging, point-of-purchase, counter-cards, posters, direct mail and/or direct response methods, paid broadcast or print advertising, special events, publicity, news conferences, give-aways, kiddie-clubs, CD ROM's, the Internet . . . if you could conceive it, and could afford it, you would do it.

The power of this total communications process is inestimable. What occurs is a synergistic effort that is larger in its scope and influence than anything any single one the three "marketing mix" disciplines can achieve on its own, or even in partnership with one or the other. To the extent that the communicator is attempting to sell a product, or a service, or an idea, integrated communication is the perfect answer.

What IC cannot do

What integrated communication cannot do is establish a reputation upon which an organization's image is based.

— Marketing and advertising are essential to establishing a brand image.

— To the degree that paid advertising is seen, heard and read, advertising still does a pretty good job.

— Marketing can help you design your product and persona, and how they are perceived by your targeted audiences.

— Public relations can use advertising to great advantage, when certain objectives must be achieved (e.g., reaching a large audience when the news media refuses to treat the organization fairly in its editorial reporting).

— Public relations uses marketing techniques to reach and influence its identified publics.

What public relations — and only public relations — can do is to lay the foundation for trust and credibility. Marketing cannot do this; advertising cannot do this. Why? Because only public relations bases its influential powers on action. Only public relations operates on the premise that "what you do speaks so loudly that I cannot hear what you say." Only credible relationships established by public relations professionals between an organization and its stakeholders can nurture an organization's reputation among its selected audiences.

Marketing is concerned with human feelings only to the extent that they cause a person to buy and use the product. Advertising is concerned with human feelings on to the extent that they respond to the message and . . . buy the product. Public relations, on the other hand, is concerned with human feelings to the extent that the relationships established can help the company change its operations and philosophies to serve more than just the company's objectives, more than just the buyer's needs, more than just the community. Public relations can (and does) work from within an organization to serve a much nobler goal — that of serving the public interest.

We are indeed the conscience of an organization. We are the ones who create the soul of an organization. Public relations alone can humanize an organization in the eyes of its stakeholders. What integrated communications does is provide some of the tools we need to do this job. Integrated communications . . . total communications . . . the marketing mix . . . when all is said and done, it really doesn't matter what it's called, as long as public relations professionals recognize that every conceivable form of communications can — and should — be used to influence desired behavior.

We need to work with the marketing and advertising people, but do not let either discipline take control of what we do, because they will forget about establishing relationships and reputation. Advertising and marketing think they know what public relations professionals do, but when it gets down to it, they have absolutely no idea what true, well-strategized public relations can do beyond supporting their own ends.

5
Propagation of Public Relations

Community Relations Programming

Sound community relations programming is predicated on three basic elements – (1) how it serves the business mission aspect of the organization, (2) how it serves the neighborhood, and (3) how it serves the organization's employees.

'Business Essential'

The primary (and often unspoken) objective of any community relations program is to serve the business strategy, to create an atmosphere of trust and understanding that will facilitate the company's growth. Altruistic motives aside, a community that is well-served and respected by the organization will be more predisposed to avail itself of the company's products and services.

How does this involvement help the organization build its business? Altruistic motives are often mentioned. The truth is that institutions become involved in their communities not only because it's the right thing to do, but because it's simply good business to do so. Participation in the business affairs of the communities served by the organization will help establish the company as a leader. That is a given. Therefore, membership in business, trade and professional associations is recommended for employees at all levels – with the stipulation that employees who are supported in their memberships must strive to become a leader in the organizations they join.

Particular attention should be paid to boards of directors composed of high-visibility business leaders. The organization should become involved in organizations that:

— Have a proven track record and a reputation for quality performance

— Have high community visibility and name recognition

— Are governed by a strong board of directors composed of influencers and top-tier leaders

— Provide opportunities for business growth

— Can help create strategic alliances

— Sponsor and initiate Innovative programs

— Target segments, demographics or geography

— Are committed to community reinvestment

— Enable the organization to increase employee participation and leadership in community

Being a Good Neighbor

Participation and support are keys to being a good neighbor. People tend to like others who do the same things they do. People tend not to fear companies that are candid and forthright about what they do. Being a good neighbor supports a myriad of values.

Being a good neighbor in both the macro sense (citizen of the state) and the local sense (citizen of the communities served) will certainly enhance the organization's corporate image and the trust that customers and neighbors have in the institution. It will increase favor with customers. It will enhance employee relations. And bottom line – it will help the community.

Important stakeholders are impacted by the good neighbor element – i.e., employees, customers, community, and investors. Good neighbor involvement comes in many forms:

— Employee volunteerism

— Employee participation in service clubs

— Employee and company participation in community organizations

— Employee and company participation in educational organizations

— Employee and company participation in nonprofit organizations

— Corporate philanthropy (giving)

— Company sponsorship of focus-related projects conducted by others

— Company ownership and sponsorship of one or more focus-related projects conducted by the organization

While it is laudable to be "all things to all people," resources are finite – there are only so many dollars, so many employees, and only so much time that can be given back to the community. Consequently, all desires to help must be tempered by a hard look at whether the involvement falls within the areas of the community relations focus.

Being a Good Employer

In a sense, the organization is a family unto itself – from executive management to middle-management to rank-and-file employees. And, extending that logic into the community, the organization's employees are the siblings, relatives, and neighbors of the area in which they work or live. Supporting employees also supports the community families' values.

A growing mode of corporate philanthropy has been to support employees in their volunteering for community and civic causes. In their monthly report, "Stakeholder Power," Walker Information notes that "Employees in the Financial Services segment gave the highest marks to the philanthropy efforts of their employees when compared to how workers in other industry groups evaluated their companies."

When companies encourage volunteerism among their employees, two things happen: First, the community's needs are met and lives are changed. Second, employees who volunteer through their work become more committed to their company because of its support. The net result is higher retention and lower turnover costs, greater motivation and productivity, and more favorable employee interactions with customers. Volunteerism fulfills ethical values, and it also adds business values as well. According to Walker Information and the Council on Foundations, employees who relate to the company's giving are more likely to act in ways that benefit the company:

— 7 out of 10 are more likely to stay with the company for at least two more years, compared to 5 out of 10 otherwise.

— 7 out of 10 are more likely to recommend their organization as a good place to work, compared to 4 out of 10 otherwise.

— 8 in 10 are more likely to do things that make customers happy, compared to 7 in 10 otherwise.

Candor is Essential in Public Relations

Here's a word that you've been hearing a lot of lately – Transparency. Simply stated, it means an organization should be open and honest about everything it does. When something – an object, a philosophy, an organization, an individual – is transparent, it means you can see through it without deflection or distortion of any kind. The concept is not new.

Public relations educators pound it into students that credibility is the stock in trade of the profession. Credibility demands transparency, candor and honesty, based on sound values, policies and actions. The issues of credibility and trust are somewhere in the middle of the Values-Image Continuum. Unless an organization acts credibly, it will not be trusted.

Political pundit Mary Matalin has noted that people now have an even lower threshold for lies and equivocation, and that there is a necessity for transparency and authenticity in what you say and how you say it. The Public Relations Coalition, in its 2003 white paper, "Restoring Trust in Business: Models for Action," suggested three concepts for restoring trust:

— Adopt ethical principles for performance

— Pursue transparency and disclosure

— Institutionalize trust and ethics, and establish formal measurement

What else can you as a public relations practitioner do? First of all, create more access and availability of information to nurture trust between your organization and its publics. Accept responsibility and commit to being held accountable for everything you do (and don't do). When you support other causes or organizations, make it known and don't keep it confidential. Here are some techniques you can use to become more transparent when you do:

— Insert a "Paid for by ..." notification in sponsored ads

— Distribute sponsorship/involvement information on your letterhead

— Use footnotes and acknowledge your involvement and support

— Issue press releases disclosing involvement in your positions; be "up front"

— List third-part involvement on your website(s)

— Insert note marks on electronic transmissions

You should ask yourself if your support is legal and the right thing to do. Remember that anything you do is fair game for the news media, and take a moment to reflect on how your activities will look in the newspapers or on television. This is not to say that you should be dissuaded from doing it, just that you should be willing to accept responsibility for anything you do. Nearly three-quarters of a century ago, Arthur Page sagely advised corporations to tell the truth and to prove it with action, because public perception is determined by what the organization does, and very little by what it says. The end goal should be honesty and accountability. Society expects it of you.

Building And Utilizing Coalitions

Strategically aligning yourself with allies is an effective way to bolster your influence in matters of public affairs and issues. There are generally two ways to do this: Partnerships, and coalitions. Partnerships involve identifying one or more companies, industries or organizations that have an affinity with your products and/or services, approaching them, and working out an agreement to your mutual benefit. Coalitions (sometimes called "alliances") are more intricate and involved, and are basically created for solidarity and mobilization. Most coalitions arise as the result of an issue (*e.g.*, legislative, social, economic, health, scientific, religious).

In many ways, coalitions have much in common with partnerships. They allow more effective and efficient delivery of persuasive advocacy, improved communication, elimination of duplication, better needs assessment, consistency of information, and increased availability of resources. They also provide "one big voice" in matters of advocacy. On the other hand, improperly managed coalitions can become ineffective if there is turf protection and mistrust, slow decision making, limited resources, diversion of resources to non-priority issues, positions adopted that are contrary to policy, and a low level of cooperation among collaborators during a crisis.

The key, therefore, is strong management. There must be a guiding force. Oftentimes it is a well-established corporation or national organization with the resources to fund an individual who coordinates activities (national, regional, state or local). This person is charged with identifying and recruiting potential allies, educating and updating them on the issue, encouraging and mobilizing their involvement when needed, serving as a resource, and managing the coalition's activities.

There are a number of arenas in which coalitions can be useful, but public affairs - the influencing of legislation and public policy - probably uses coalitions to the greatest extent. The task of the coordinator is to persuade coalition members to articulate their support or opposition to the proposed legislation in a persuasive manner, delivered on a timely basis to the legislators holding key positions. Initial contact with the legislator sometimes comes from the coordinator, but as a general rule, once the coalition is formed, the coordinator facilitates ally contacts instead of participating in the dialogue.

Who do you want in your coalition? Your friends. And maybe, your enemies. Put aside your emotional involvement in hot issues, and concentrate on the strategic goal of your effort. There is a saying among gamblers - "Bet smart, not your heart." The same applies here. Recruit anybody who can help you with *this particular issue.* You don't have to be their friends afterwards, just band together for the common cause. Essentially, you want coalition members who are not afraid to speak out on issues, who can look past emotion and focus on logic and practicality.

A good place to start is the Yellow Pages. Look under "Associations." Call your Chamber of Commerce and ask them for a directory (you may have to pay a fee if you are not a member). Put on your thinking cap and expand your frame of reference; practically every trade, professional or special interest group is a potential ally, but only if you can make your cause relevant to theirs in some way.

One very effective strategy is to recruit trade associations. A dozen allies can speak individually and as a coalition, but they bring with them a much greater resource - their own memberships. They can speak on behalf of the membership, or, hopefully, they can mobilize their members and deliver support by the hundreds or thousands . Associations are what are PR calls "special audiences," because they are organized and can communicate with their members more efficiently and faster than you can if you had to approach them individually.

Provide your allies with the information (ammunition) they need to articulate their view intelligently. Regular communication is very important, whether it be a quarterly gathering, a periodic newsletter, individual phonecalls and meetings, or attending your coalition allies' social and special interest functions. And it should go without saying that whenever possible, you must go out of your way to help them (*e.g.* drafting letters, doing basic research, answering questions, providing solutions for their problems, and options for intelligent decisions).

Generally speaking, coalition coordinators sometimes should not be lobbyists. Lobbyists are a specialized group who operate entirely within the legislative and political arenas. Coalition coordinators' work will cross party lines and involve a wide variety of allies with diverse political and economic interests. Therefore, remaining politically neutral might be of advantage. But if an issue is important enough to your industry and you require the services of a lobbyist to protect your interests in municipal, state and federal government, then hire the best lobbyist you can find. This is another case where "as good as" does not justify anything less than "excellent," especially where thousands of jobs and millions of dollars are at stake. And don't forget to make the lobbyist part of your coalition team.

Communications Audits

A communications audit can be a useful tool when it comes to analyzing the effectiveness of an organization's persuasive messages - both within and without the organization. While it is not a panacea, it can identify logjams, interference and excessive message-garbling noise that will dilute communications effectiveness.

— The process in brief is:

— Ask a lot of questions

— Listen carefully to the answers

— Determine the most effective and efficient ways to overcome the barriers

— Analyze existing communications tools

— Eliminate those that aren't working

— Identify and install initiatives that will work

Internal Interviews

Interview a cross-section of employees (line, staff and administrative) in sufficient numbers to validate response trends. Interview at least 25% of all employees, to a maximum of 150 or so to keep your audit manageable. If the employee pool is 50 or less (small business size), talk to them all. You should talk to representative numbers of employees at every level. Be sure to talk to ALL management people, including line supervisors. It's interesting how upper levels of management have entirely different perceptions from operational employees of how effective their communications efforts are.

You are trying to discover flaws in the internal system. Ask probing open-ended questions such as:

— Are you getting all the information you want to do your job well? Is there anything you want that you're not getting?

— Are memoranda and announcements easily understood? Could you give me some examples?

— How do you get updates on what's happening in the company? In your department?

— What does, and doesn't, work with your present communications set-up? How would you improve it?

— If you wanted to give feedback or suggestions, how do you do it now?

— Does the feedback/suggestion procedure work? If it doesn't, how would you improve it?

— Whom do you believe more - your co-workers, your immediate supervisor, department managers, division heads, or the "boss"?

— Do you talk about your work or the organization outside of your job? What do you say?

External Interviews

With external audiences, you must first identify the important "thought leaders" - the people whose ideas and perceptions count, and who influence the opinions of others. These "infuentials" will include people from the business community, chambers of commerce, political leaders, association directors, community activists, government leaders (both elective and bureaucratic), news media, the organization's suppliers and purveyors, unions, professional organizations, education (public and private; primary, secondary and collegiate) - in other words, just about anybody whose opinion counts when you're trying to infuence behavior.

The line of questioning for external audiences examines reputation and perception, and validates the link in the Action-Image continuum:

— Action: Good, responsible action on the part of the organization creates an atmosphere of Trust.

— Trust: When people trust you, they will listen; and when they listen, you gain Credibility.

— Credibility: If you are believed to be credible, your Reputation grows.

— Reputation: Your reputation is your good name, which you've worked hard to earn. Don't blow it. If you have a good reputation, you'll have a good Image in people's minds.

— Image: The "public" and your stakeholders will see you in a good light; your organization will benefit and flourish, enabling you to institute more needed Action

All interviews should be one-on-one, face-to-face; anonymity must be guaranteed or responses will be biased. Anonymity is critical, so for internal interviews, ask for a comfortable room that allows privacy. A room with comfortable furniture is ideal (sofa and easy chairs instead of desk and hard chairs). The interviewer must be trusted, so dress appropriately (in other words, do not overdress), because people tend to trust people who look and act like them. Spend a couple of days just wandering around and talking to management and employees on an informal basis. This gives everybody a chance to at least "size you up" and familiarize themselves with your presence.

ALINSKY'S RULES FOR RADICALS

To paraphrase some sage advice, "keep your friends close, keep your enemies closer." If your business or organization ever becomes a target of radical activists, it will be extremely helpful to know what strategies of attack will used against you. Short of having spies infiltrate their organization - a practice that is sure to be found out and exposed to your discredit - it would help to study their methods.

Known as the "father of modern American radicalism," Saul D. Alinsky developed strategies and tactics that take the enormous, unfocused emotional energy of grassroots groups and transform it into effective anti-government and anti-corporate activism. Activist organizations teach his ideas widely taught today as a set of model behaviors, and they use these principles to create an emotional commitment to victory - no matter what. Grassroots pressure on large organizations is reality, and there is every indication that it will grow. Because the conflicts manifest in high-profile public debate and often-panicked decision-making, studying Alinsky's rules will help organizations develop counteractive strategies that can level the playing field.

Governments and corporations have inherent weaknesses. And, time and again, they repeat mistakes that other large organizations have made, even repeating their own mistakes. Alinsky's out-of-print book - "Rules for Radicals" - illustrates why opposition groups take on large organizations with utter glee, and why these governments and corporations fail to win. Large organizations have learned to stonewall and not empower activists. In other words, they try to ignore radical activists and are never as committed to victory as their opposition is committed to defeating them. They are unprepared for the hailstorm of brutal tactics that severely damage their reputation and send them running with their tails between their legs.

Some of these rules are ruthless, but they work. Here are the rules to be aware of:

1. "Power is not only what you have, but what the enemy thinks you have." Power is derived from 2 main sources - money and people. "Have-Nots" must build power from flesh and blood. (These are two things of which there is a plentiful supply. Government and corporations always have a difficult time appealing to people, and usually do so almost exclusively with economic arguments.)

2. "Never go outside the expertise of your people." It results in confusion, fear and retreat. Feeling secure adds to the backbone of anyone. (Organizations under attack wonder why radicals don't address the "real" issues. This is why. They avoid things with which they have no knowledge.)

3. "Whenever possible, go outside the expertise of the enemy." Look for ways to increase insecurity, anxiety and uncertainty. (This happens all the time. Watch how many organizations under attack are blind-sided by seemingly irrelevant arguments that they are then forced to address.)

4. "Make the enemy live up to its own book of rules." If the rule is that every letter gets a reply, send 30,000 letters. You can kill them with this because no one can possibly obey all of their own rules. (This is a serious rule. The besieged entity's very credibility and reputation is at stake, because if activists catch it lying or not living up to its commitments, they can continue to chip away at the damage.)

5. "Ridicule is man's most potent weapon." There is no defense. It's irrational. It's infuriating. It also works as a key pressure point to force the enemy into concessions. (Pretty crude, rude and mean, huh? They want to create anger and fear.)

6. "A good tactic is one your people enjoy." They'll keep doing it without urging and come back to do more. They're doing their thing, and will even suggest better ones. (Radical activists, in this sense, are no different that any other human being. We all avoid "un-fun" activities, and but we revel at and enjoy the ones that work and bring results.)

7. "A tactic that drags on too long becomes a drag." Don't become old news. (Even radical activists get bored. So to keep them excited and involved, organizers are constantly coming up with new tactics.)

8. "Keep the pressure on. Never let up." Keep trying new things to keep the opposition off balance. As the opposition masters one approach, hit them from the flank with something new. (Attack, attack, attack from all sides, never giving the reeling organization a chance to rest, regroup, recover and re-strategize.)

9. "The threat is usually more terrifying than the thing itself." Imagination and ego can dream up many more consequences than any activist. (Perception is reality. Large organizations always prepare a worst-case scenario, something that may be furthest from the activists' minds. The upshot is that the organization will expend enormous time and energy, creating in its own collective mind the direst of conclusions. The possibilities can easily poison the mind and result in demoralization.)

10. "If you push a negative hard enough, it will push through and become a positive." Violence from the other side can win the public to your side because the public sympathizes with the underdog. (Unions used this tactic. Peaceful [albeit loud] demonstrations during the heyday of unions in the early to mid-20th Century incurred management's wrath, often in the form of violence that eventually brought public sympathy to their side.)
11. "The price of a successful attack is a constructive alternative." Never let the enemy score points because you're caught without a solution to the problem. (Old saw: If you're not part of the solution, you're part of the problem. Activist organizations have an agenda, and their strategy is to hold a place at the table, to be given a forum to wield their power. So, they have to have a compromise solution.)
12. Pick the target, freeze it, personalize it, and polarize it." Cut off the support network and isolate the target from sympathy. Go after people and not institutions; people hurt faster than institutions. (This is cruel, but very effective. Direct, personalized criticism and ridicule works.)

Achieving Societal Alignment

"Societal alignment" is one of those buzz-phrases that pops up every now and then – like "integrated communication," or "constructive engagement." Truth be told? This is not much more than the good, old-fashioned two-way symmetrical model of public relations. There are four basic public relations models, as enumerated by Jim Grunig and Todd Hunt in their text, *Managing Public Relations*:

— *Press agentry*: We only tell them what we want them to hear, we sell the story to the news media and the publics we want to influence.

— *Public information*: We tell them everything we know, and let them make up their own minds.

— *Two-way asymmetrical*: We let them talk back to us (feedback), then we use that information to craft our message and make it more attractive and persuasive.

— *Two-way symmetrical*: We talk with them, and use their feedback to improve our product or service, and more importantly, to change the way we do our business in order to benefit them.

Servicing the public (servicing society, that is) requires good management of expectations – not our expectations, but the expectations of those we serve. But we can't do that unless we're 'way ahead of the curve, unless we make sure that we know exactly what it is that our society expects of us and what we produce and do for them, and how they expect us to behave in the process.

It starts with research. It starts with listening. It continues with gaining a profound understanding of what we hear. We need to strive for a greater understanding of what society expects of us. It is most important that we listen to those expectations, then apply those very expectations to the way we manage our business.

Two-way communication is imperative in the two-way symmetrical model. Talk "with" and not just "to" the constituencies. At this point in aligning ourselves with society, our job is not to educate, it is instead to learn. Our job is not to advocate, it is to be sincere in our desire to meet expectations. Our job is not to persuade, it is to change. Who we talk with is important – thought leaders, those who influence opinions in others, those who have a handle on where society is headed, those who use our products, those who avail themselves of our services. We know who the specific publics are for our organization. Let's talk with them.

Finally, when all of the research and feedback has been organized and digested, it is important to strategize a platform that we can use to manage the issues we've uncovered. Our messages – and more importantly, our business practices – can then be adapted with this new-found knowledge, in order that we become more aligned with society. Some call understanding, communicating, and adapting the "Three Pillars of Societal Alignment."

Within the framework of these three pillars, use every tool available, including formal and informal research, strategic planning, improvement and enhancement of current and new skills through professional development, use of state-of-the-art technology as a communications and outreach tool, and logistical and philosophical coordination. How do we reach the goals and objectives we've set in the beginning when we first ideated aligning ourselves with society?

Strategically selected tactics, that's how. Some communication-oriented, some action-oriented. Remember now, the ultimate goal is to change ourselves, not just what we say. Reach out to those whose opinions count. But don't forget that in societal alignment, we need to slip into lock-step with everybody who has an opinion, everyone who has the power to affect the environment in which we operate. And since Congress makes the laws of the land that regulate what we can and cannot do, it stands to reason that every voter, every tax-paying citizen, every potential taxpayer or voter, is whom we should be listening to at some point. It's that vast, amorphous group of people known as the "general public" with whom we are aligning.

Engaging in a proactive, constructive dialog with opponents is critical, as we listen carefully to their concerns and seek common ground. We can work on building our image through changed and more socially acceptable behavior, maintaining honest and open channels of communication. Changed behavior can translate into credibility, trust, and inevitably, an improved reputation that will lay the ground work for an improved image.

Every stakeholder is important – e.g., employees, shareholders, investors, customers and clients, purveyors, communities in which we reside and/or operate, government. Being aligned internally is a vital necessity. Employees, consultants, partners all have to be on the same page to avoid confusion and misdirection. Maintain a constant, open and honest dialog with employees. If we are to continue to exist as viable organizations, then we need to able to pull ourselves into alignment with society, which after all, has power to make us obsolete. For if we become obsolete, then the good things we can do for society will not come to pass.

6

Participatory Public Relations

Participation has been a fundamental component of the Internet since its inception. Newsgroups, mailing lists and bulletin boards were the early cousins to the forums, weblogs and collaborative communities flourishing today. Those early forms are still thriving, a testament to our need to stay connected to our social networks. Participatory journalism flourishes in social media - the interpersonal communication that takes place through email, chat, message boards, forums - and in collaborative media - hybrid forms of news, discussion and community.

This section categorizes the forms in which participatory journalism takes shape. Some of these forms continue to evolve and merge and thus overlap. The list, while generalized, is meant to describe the outlines of that participation and the communities where it resides. Considering the "publish, then filter" model that most of these forms follow, we define each form's self-correcting or filtering mechanism. The end goal of filtering is the same in all - to amplify the signal-to-noise ratio, separating the meaningful information from the chatter.

Different Forms of Participatory Journalism

Discussion groups

Online discussion groups are the oldest and still the most popular forms for participation. Discussion groups run the gamut from bulletin boards and forums to mailing lists and chat rooms. Participants might engage a discussion group to answer tech support questions, to trade stock-trading tips, to argue about a favorite sports team, to share experiences about a health care issue, or to join a collaborative work project.

Mailing lists, newsgroups, bulletin boards, and forums are methods of asynchronous communication, meaning that all participants do not have to be online at the same time to communicate. Sometimes this leads to more thoughtful contributions, because participants have more time to refine their responses. Chat rooms, on the other hand, are synchronous, where all participants must be online at the same time to communicate. This has the benefit of providing immediacy and can be used effectively for business services such as customer support. But for the most part, chat rooms are more like virtual cafes or hangouts, with live, unfiltered discussion.

Forum discussions are probably the most familiar discussion group form to the average Internet user. Forums are typically arranged into threads in which an initial message or post appears at the beginning of a discussion and responses are attached in a branching manner. When forums are viewed in threads, it's easy to recognize the branching of conversation that occurs, some of which might not be entirely related to the original post. Some forums permit the audience to sort messages by various means - popularity, date, ranking. Many forums are archived, turning them into a searchable knowledge base of community conversation.

Strengths and weaknesses of various forms of online participation are described below;

Self-correcting process: In a discussion group, moderators police the content and actions of participants, sometimes removing and editing parts of the conversations that violate the standards of the community. These moderators are sometimes appointed by the community; in other cases they are appointed by the host or owner of the forums. However, in many discussion communities, the participants police each other, sharing their views of when particular behaviors or actions are inappropriate.

Strengths: Most discussion forms have a relatively low barrier to entry (just create an user account), with an especially low level of commitment. For example, a participant can engage a forum only once, or few times, and still have a meaningful experience.

Weaknesses: Sometimes forums are too open, easily garnering flip, reactive comments. Active, large forums can get noisy, with so many posts from so many members, it's hard to determine what information is meaningful or useful. In addition, some moderated forums require each post to be pre-approved before it appears online, slowing down and smothering the conversation.

Many online media outlets have abandoned discussion forums in the past few years, citing legal problems as well as lack of sufficient staff to moderate and maintain forums. Ultimately, some media outlets think forums provide little value to the audience and to the bottom line (ROI). One barrier to effective advertising on these pages is the lack of content control by either the advertiser or publisher.

User-generated content

Many news sites provide a vehicle - through Web-based forms or email - designed to collect content from the audience and redistribute it. This vehicle can collect full-length articles, advice/tips, journals, reviews, calendar events, useful links, photos and more. The content is usually text-based, but increasingly we are seeing the contribution of audio, video and photographs. After submission, the content appears online with or without editorial review, depending on the nature of content and the host policy.

Ranking is another popular and easy way for the audience to participate. Examples include rating a story, a reporter and other users. Ranking systems typically provide the best benefit when a sufficient number of users have participated, for example, "4,202 readers give this movie 4 out of 5 stars." Internet users also provide content through feedback systems, such as polls or mini-forums attached to story pages. Polls sometimes also support comment submissions.

Self-correcting process: Usually, audience submissions go to a traditional editor at the host site, undergo an editing or approval process, and then are posted to the Web. Ranking and feedback mechanisms, however, are typically posted live immediately. Communities often police the submissions, and strong agreement or disagreement with a submission may prompt members to submit their own comments. This commonly occurs with reviews of products, movies and restaurants.

Strengths: Like forums, audience submissions have a relatively low barrier to entry, with a low level of commitment. A participant can submit (usually on topics that meet a special interest) only once, or few times, and still have a meaningful experience. Those who post repeatedly may build up over time a reputation among their peers as an expert on the subject.

Weaknesses: The quality of user-generated content can be uneven, with participants who are not trained writers or fact-checkers. As a result, some content can require extensive editing. Generally, this type of content relies on the good will of the audience to not exploit the system. It's easy, in some cases, to skew polls and other feedback systems, by voting multiple times. Also, a low volume of participation can limit the value of feedback systems.

Weblogs

Among the newest forms of participatory journalism to gain popularity is the weblog. A weblog is a web page made up of usually short, frequently updated text blocks or entries that are arranged in reverse chronological order (most recent to oldest). The content and purpose of weblogs vary greatly, ranging from personal diary to journalistic community news to collaborative discussion groups in a corporate setting.

Weblogs can provide links and commentary about content on other Web sites. They can be a form of "latest news" page. Or they can consist of project diaries, photos, poetry, mini-essays, project updates, even fiction. The quick, short posts on weblogs have been likened to "instant messages to the Web." Weblogs fall into the one-to-many (individual blogs) or many-to-many (group blogs) model of media, with some allowing no or little discussion by users and others generating robust reader responses. Either way, weblogs inevitably become part of what is now called the "blogosphere." This is the name given to the intercast of weblogs - the linking to and discussion of what others have written or linked to, in essence a distributed discussion.

The blogosphere is facilitated by several technologies. First, it is supported by TrackBack - a mechanism that automatically finds other comments about a blog post on a weblog, and provides excerpts and links to the comments alongside the post. It's like having an editorial page of commentary on the Web, automatically generated to appear alongside a story. Second, the blogosphere is fueled by meta-sites such as Daypop, MIT's Blogdex, Technorati and others. Theses sites track what items weblogs are linking to and talking about - news stories, weblog posts, new products (movies, books, software), whatever subject is catching their attention. Meta-sites provides a popularity ranking of the most linked-to items, and then indexes all links to those items.

The blogosphere is also supported by a third technology, XML or RSS syndication. This allows weblogs to syndicate their content to anyone using a "news reader," a downloadable program that creates a peer-to-peer distribution model. With content so easily exchanged, it's easy to know what others in your peer group are talking about. Weblogs are a powerful draw in that they enable the individual participant to play multiple roles simultaneously - publisher, commentator, moderator, writer, documentarian.

Weblogs have also proven to be effective collaborative communication tools. They help small groups (and in a few cases, large) communicate in a way that is simpler and easier to follow than email lists or discussion forums. A collaborative weblog can help keep everyone in the loop, promoting cohesiveness in the group.

Self-correcting process: Weblogs rely on audience feedback, through weblog commenting forms, email or remarks made on other weblogs, as a method of correction.

Typically, webloggers are reliable about correcting their mistakes, and a great many frequently link to dissenting viewpoints on the Web.

Strengths: Weblogs are easy to set up, operate and maintain. The technology is relatively inexpensive, sometimes even free. This allows just about anyone to simultaneously become a publisher, creator and distributor of content.

Weaknesses: This type of publishing requires a higher level of commitment and time from the creator than other forms. Also, it is difficult for weblogs to attract readers, other than through word of mouth and weblog aggregation and search engines. Weblogs have also been judged as being too self-referential, with critics likening them more to the "Daily Me" than the "Daily We."

Collaborative publishing

The technology behind many online communities is open source and free. In addition, Web publishing tools and content management systems are becoming easier to install, deploy and manage. As a result, thousands of Web-based collaborative publishing communities have appeared in the past five years. As open-source tools for forums, weblogs and content management systems (CMS) have evolved, they have begun to blur into each other. This has led to the development of groupware, Web- or desktop-based applications designed for the collaborative creation and distribution of news and information, file-sharing and communication.

Weblogs are considered to be groupware, because they can be collaboratively created. But in this section, we are addressing systems that are somewhat more complex. A collaborative publishing environment is designed to enable a group of participants (large or small) to play multiple roles: content creators, moderators, editors, advertisers and readers. While the environment may be owned by an individual creator or host organization, the goal of these systems is distributed ownership and deep involvement from its community of users.

Forums, mailing lists and weblogs can be effective collaborative publishing environments. But what distinguishes this group from other forms is the self-correcting process and the rules that govern participation. Forums use moderators and community feedback. Weblogs usually have a feedback feature or, more often, other weblogs link back and discuss posts. However, in complex collaborative publishing environments, the self-correcting processes are more akin to peer review, traditional editing oversight and meta-moderators, individuals who police moderators to make sure the conversation doesn't get skewed or diluted.

The most well-known of these environments is Slashdot.org, which resembles a cross between a large-scale forum and a collaborative weblog. Slashdot is driven by a combination of editorial oversight by its owners, submissions by users, and moderation and meta-moderation by the community of users. The site attracts more than 10 million unique readers each month, with roughly a half million audience members (5 percent) participating by submitting articles, moderating, ranking and posting comments. The open-source technology behind Slashdot now runs thousands of similar communities on the Web.

Extending the Slashdot model in a different direction, Kuroshin.org passed on editorial oversight to its members.

Every story is written by a member and then submitted for peer review. Next, the story is edited, discussed and ranked before it even appears on the site. Finally, the audience reacts, comments and extends the story. The open-source technology that runs Kuroshin, called Scoop, is a "collaborative media application" according to its creator, Rusty Foster. "It empowers your visitors to be the producers of the site, to contribute news and discussion, and to make sure the signal remains high."

One measure of the success of these two collaboration systems is that Google News includes Slashdot and Kuroshin as two of the 4,500 sources for its news search index. A somewhat less-structured approach to collaborative publishing is the Wiki model. Wiki technology, depending on how its deployed, is used for writing, discussion, storage, email and collaboration. Wikipedia is an international, open content, collaboratively developed encyclopedia. In just over two years, it has amassed more than 120,000 articles in English as well as more than 75,000 articles in other languages.

At first glance, a Wiki appears to be somewhat chaotic, allowing any member the ability to create public domain articles and edit just about any piece of text within the environment. The central component is that every change is tracked, and can be reviewed, challenged or restored - an omnipotent version history. As evidence to the ever-blurring lines of these forms, there are now experiments in Wiki-style weblogs. Another interesting example of a collaborative publishing is Zaplet technology, where discussion forums, polling and group decision-making tools are exchanged inside dynamic emails.

Among the most advanced and ambitious groupware desktop applications is Groove, created by Ray Ozzie, who also created one of the best-known collaboration tools, Lotus Notes. Groove is a peer-to-peer program that allows large or small groups to collaboratively write, surf, exchange files, chat, create forums and invite outsiders to participate. It even supports voice-over-IP communications.

Self-correcting process: Collaborative systems usually have a detailed workflow for built-in correction, such as Slashdot's system, where the audience ranks other audience members and their comments, moderators police discussions, and moderators are monitored by meta-moderators. In the case of Kuroshin, the audience acts as editor before and after publishing.

Strengths: Participants can engage multiple roles, or earn the privilege of new roles. A greater level of involvement and ownership from the audience usually yields greater reward (better discussion and content) than in other forms.

Weaknesses: These systems are more difficult to launch and maintain than others, due to technical complexity. Depending on the number of participants in the environment, the speed at which membership grows, and how active the membership is in creating content, collaborative systems become increasingly unwieldy and complex to manage.

Peer-to-Peer

Peer-to-peer (P2P) describes applications in which people can use the Internet to communicate or share and distribute digital files with each other directly or through a mediating Web server. P2P communication: Instant Messaging (IM) and Short Message Service (SMS) are the most pervasive forms of peer-to-peer communication. These forms constitute types of social media, where personal, informal conversation occurs in a "one-to-one" or "one-to-few" model.

While the content of IM and SMS is difficult to categorize or analyze, its appeal and usefulness as a communications medium is unquestionable. Surveys from the Pew Internet and American Life Project reveal that more than 50 million Americans (about 46 percent of all Internet users) have send instant messages, and about 7 million (11 percent) of all these users send instant messages daily. AOL, one of the most popular of instant messaging providers, transmits almost 1.4 billion instant messages each day.

SMS, short text messages that are sent between cell phones, is pervasive in Europe and Asia but hasn't yet gained traction in the United States due to the lack of support for a key industry technology (GSM). In the past decade, as American culture has embraced mobile technologies, instant messaging has become a powerful means of distributing news and information to computers, cell phones, pagers and PDAs. Now, everything from news headlines and stories, sports scores, stock quotes, airline flight schedules and eBay bids are regularly sent directly to mobile devices, through instant messages or SMS.

In addition, parents keep in closer contact with their teen children through IM. Reuters explored the business prospects for instant messaging of news, sports and financial information with an ActiveBuddy tool. Audience members who added this intelligent news agent as a IM buddy could ask for news on demand based on keywords. In Hong Kong, the Chinese government sent a blanket of 6 million SMS messages to spread the word and avert panic about the outbreak of the SARS respiratory illness.

As cell phones and mobile devices have integrated digital camera technology, instant messaging is now expanding outside of text communications to include still photography and video. This is already being used in a peer-to-peer fashion among friends or colleagues, but it is also being used as a vehicle to submit photography and video directly to a Web site or weblog. During worldwide protests against the war in Iraq, the BBCNews.com asked its readers to submit photos from their digital cameras and cell phones. Microsoft's ThreeDegrees application is an interesting experiment in peer-to-peer communication. Participants form groups with this software to chat, share pictures and music to the group, without permanently sharing the files. Music and images are streamed to the group members on the fly.

P2P Distribution: Peer-to-peer forms excel when it comes to the distribution and dissemination of digital files, which may carry valuable news and information. Instant messaging users can exchange digital files on the fly in the middle of a conversation. But the heart of P2P file sharing was born with Napster, the controversial desktop software program designed to enable participants to share any digital music file on their hard drives. At its zenith, 70 million users were trading 2.7 billion files per month. Since Napster was shut down, other file-sharing programs (called Gnutella clients) such as Morpheus and Kazaa have stepped in, allowing billions of movies, songs, ebooks, software and other digital files to be exchanged among the masses.

From a participatory journalism perspective, P2P has enormous potential to distribute the content created by digital amateurs. One example is the recent emergence of P2P photo-sharing software programs. Such programs let you define a list of friends and mark photos that you want to share with your them. The program watches for your friends to log on and then automatically makes the images available for downloading or real-time viewing.

Self-correcting process: Peer-to-peer file sharing doesn't necessarily need correction, but ranking and filtering mechanisms can increase the signal-to-noise ratio. Peer-to-peer communication such as instant messaging doesn't need correction either, any more than a conversation with a friend would. However, chat rooms sometimes benefit from moderation.

Strengths: Synchronous communication is a powerful vehicle for immediate news and information. SMS has the advantage of being both synchronous and asynchronous, because if a participant isn't online, the message is stored for later retrieval.

Weaknesses: Instant messaging requires participants to be online in order to communicate. The lack of interoperability between software programs, conflicting messaging standards and closed devices are sources of continual frustration, creating islands of users who are unable communicate with others. For example, an AOL instant messaging user cannot communicate with an MSN user.

XML syndication

The content on many of these forms, especially blogs and collaborative systems, can be syndicated through the use of an XML specification called RSS, Rich Site Summary. An RSS file typically contains a list of headlines, summaries and links recently published by a given site. Using news reader applications such as NewzCrawler, AmphetaDesk or NetNewsWire, Web readers can browse these RSS files, sorting through large amounts of news content at a rapid rate. When a reader finds an item of interest, she clicks on the headline and it takes her to the story on the source's site.

RSS syndication seems to be making an impact in several ways. Content creators, from mainstream media to the average blogger, can easily syndicate their content to RSS reader applications, creating a peer-to-peer distribution model. In many cases, the user doesn't have to do a thing. "It's all part of the democratization effect of the Web," says entrepreneur Dave Winer, who incorporated an early version of RSS in Userland blogging software in 1999. "It puts bloggers on the same field as the big news corporations, and that's great."

News readers can be trained to go out and refresh content based on a time schedule. This allows readers to be up to date without having to search for recent news on their own. "Most people, once they start using RSS to check the news, just don't go back (to surfing Web pages)," says Tim Bray, co-editor of the World Wide Web Consortium's XML specification. "The amount of time and irritation saved is totally, completely addictive."

According to columnist J.D. Lasica, this virtue can motivate users into an immediate online dialogue, whether through e-mails, discussion boards or blog entries. Interactivity is much more vibrant when the news is fresh. News readers help to build community. You can see the ebb and flow of ideas around the network much better now. The XML structure of RSS feeds also allows other sites to easily integrate a headline and summary feed into other products, redistributing content in a viral fashion.

Open vs. closed

The scale of these forms, the technology behind them and type of participation that occurs varies greatly. However, the nature of participation can be affected by one additional key factor that should be considered: Is the environment public or private? We have identified four categories of openness that these forms usually fall within:

1. *Open Communal*: While there typically is a single host, facilitator or architect of the community, almost all activity within it - membership, editing, filtering, moderation, content contribution, etc. - is managed and governed by the community it serves.
2. *Open Exclusive*: A group of privileged members, usually the owners of the site, is allowed to post primary content to the site, while the audience creates secondary content through commentary. This is typical of weblogs. Sometimes exclusivity can be assigned to audience members. For example, MetaFilter limits the number of new members that can join each day.
3. *Closed*: Only a group of privileged members can read, post, edit and comment on content. The system, which can take the form of a weblog or forum, exists in a private Web environment, such as a company intranet. Instant messaging and email are private, and thus closed.
4. *Partially Closed*: In this case, some portion of the information created by a closed community is exposed to a public Web space.

Functions of Participation

This section categorize participatory journalism by the function the audience serves.

Commentary

The most pervasive, and perhaps fundamental, level of

participation is commentary. During the past three decades, forums, newsgroups, chat rooms and instant messaging have enabled online discussion on just about any subject of interest imaginable. Summing up the ubiquity and popularity of this activity, a Pew Research report noted that in the days following the Sept. 11 attacks, nearly one-third of all American Internet users "read or posted material in chat rooms, bulletin boards or online forums."

In the past five years, weblogs have increased the signal of this activity, with some advocating the blog form as the next generation of newspaper op/ed page. "Though webloggers do actual reporting from time to time, most of what they bring to the table is opinion and analysis - punditry," says Glenn Reynolds, a law professor at the University of Tennessee and author of the popular weblog InstaPundit.

Filtering and editing

With the flood of information available, as well as competing demands of media attention, the door has opened for alternative forms of editing - filtering, sorting, ranking and linking. This process is akin to "editing" in the sense of editorial judgment and selection. The online participants "guide and direct" their community, large or small, to valued news and information. Filtering and ranking can be based on explicit singular or collective participation. For example, Gizmodo, "the Gadgets Weblog," is a well-edited, "best-of" list of links to news and information about cutting-edge consumer electronics. Gizmodo is produced by one person. The search engine Daypop, also run by one person, has a collection of the Top most linked-to news and information Web pages within the blogging community.

Many news sites, such as MSNBC.com and CNN.com, employ a similar "Most Read Top 10," where all site visitors' choices are accumulated into a popularity ranking. Other interesting examples of filtering systems include Google's Page Rank algorithms, Yahoo's Buzz - based on popular searches - and The New York Times' "most e-mailed stories." Filtering, however, doesn't have to come from explicit activities, such as linking or favorite lists. It can also have implicit origins, such as Amazon's well-known "People who bought this item also bought..." feature. This is an example of collaborative filtering, in which Amazon uses information about previous sales and browsing to suggest potentially relevant products to returning customers.

Fact-checking

In discussion forums and weblogs, the act of verification is a frequent activity. The initial post in either form begins with a link to a story, followed by a statement questioning the validity of certain facts. What ensues is a community effort to uncover the truth. Sometimes journalists enter the fray in an effort to uncover the truth in traditional media. One example of this occurred when the Slashdot community and an Associated Press reporter uncovered a fraudulent ad campaign by Microsoft. "This is tomorrow's journalism," says blogger and journalist Dan Gillmor, "a partnership of sorts between professionals and the legions of gifted amateurs out there who can help us - all of us - figure things out. It's a positive development, and we're still figuring out how it works."

Grassroots reporting

Taking the form of eyewitness or first-hand accounts, Internet users are participating in the fact-gathering and reporting process, sometimes even conveying breaking news. Weblogs and forums brought compelling first-hand accounts and photography to the events of September 11. The terrorist attacks were the watershed event for grassroots reporting in weblogs, says John Hiler, co-founder of WebCrimson, a software consulting firm based in Manhattan, and Xanga.com, one of the largest weblog community sites. "Eyewitness reporting comes in large part from people's desire to share their stories and publish the truth. These are key features in blog-based grassroots reporting, and a big reason that weblogs have exploded in popularity since September 11th."

"There are so many post 9-11 weblogs that they've gotten their own name: warblogs," Hiler says. Warblogs continue to dissect and analyze the news from the war on terrorism. The scope of blog journalism has expanded to other areas of interest. "Alternative internet sources are gaining a reputation for breaking important news stories more quickly than traditional media sources," says Chris Sherman, associate editor of SearchEngineWatch.com. "For example, The New York Times reported that the first hint of problems that doomed the space shuttle Columbia appeared on an online discussion eleven minutes before the Associated Press issued its first wire-service alert."

Fact-gathering and grassroots reporting also come from professional or amateur subject matter experts who publish a weblog or participate in a collaborative community, such as Slashdot. These participants tend to produce a wealth of original content as well as opinion, links and original databases of resources on their expertise. This is particularly successful on a subject or theme that is not covered well by mainstream media. An excellent example of such niche amateurs is the Web site Digital Photography Review. This news and reviews site is written and produced by UK photography consultant Phil Askey and his wife Joanna. The nearly 4-year-old site features a weblog on digital photography news, plus in-depth equipment reviews and original coverage of trade shows. It also has a active discussion forum. From its modest beginnings in late 1998, it now attracts almost 7 million unique visitors and 40 million page views each month.

Annotative reporting

Another way to characterize the fact-checking, grassroots reporting and commentary in weblogs and related forms is to view the activity as an extension of traditional reportage. Adding to, or supplementing, the information in a given story is the goal of many participants who believe that a particular point of view, angle or piece of information is missing from coverage in the mainstream media. Reporters have also used participatory forms on the web to annotate themselves, calling it "transparent journalism," by publishing the complete text of their interviews on their weblogs.

Open-source journalism

Some media are allowing their readers to evaluate and react to content online before its official publication in the traditional product. Journalism researcher Mark Deuze suggests that this type of journalism, similar to a peer review process, is best suited to "specialized niche markets" whose audience has comparably specialized interests and needs. Considering the fluidity and connectivity of the Internet, it is within reason to suggest that a community of interested peers could quickly be assembled on any given subject.

Audio/Video broadcasting

While not nearly as widespread due to cost barriers and technological know-how, the Web has empowered the audience to the play the role of audio or video broadcaster. Internet radio and television stations use streaming servers or straight file downloads to deliver content. These bandwidth-intensive sites can be expensive to operate and require donations or some type of revenue stream to survive. Yet thousands of these sites continue to thrive, like many audience-driven sites, by providing alternative/niche content. As broadband adoption increases, creation tools get cheaper and more simple, and the entertainment center of the home (TV) gets connected to the Web, we should see a significant proliferation of audio and video content created and distributed by the audience.

Buying, selling and advertising

The egalitarian ethos driving participatory journalism is not restricted merely to the dissemination of news and information but also encompasses commerce and advertising. The web has created an unprecedented opportunity for consumers to openly discuss the products that fill their lives. From email to web sites to Usenet, there are millions of conversations on anything and everything you can buy, rent, or do. Commerce communities began to develop in the mid-'90s with sites such as Amazon, which include reviews by users on its product pages. Sites like Edmunds.com provide discussion and advice about purchasing cars. The participation in commerce communities includes commentary, grassroots reporting and fact-checking.

At the same time, in the mid-'90s, consumer to consumer (C2C) environments began to establish the notion of the audience owning all aspects of the business chain - buying and selling to each other. Examples range from the monolithic auction site eBay, with more than 12 million items for sale, to the intimate, down-to-earth classifieds of craigslist.org.

Easy-to-use systems such as PayPal, Amazon zShops and Yahoo Stores enable any Internet user to put up a storefront in a few hours. Affiliate programs, like those set up by Amazon, allow anyone to share in the profits when an item sells. Donation engines, like Amazon's Honor System, enable small-scale publishers like webloggers to collect an income ranging from the modest to respectable. During a one-week pledge drive in December 2002, weblogger and New Republic senior editor Andrew Sullivan generated $79,020 in donations from 3,339 of his weblog readers.

In the past few years, following the lead of Google and collaborative weblogs such as MetaFilter and Kuroshin, we have begun to see the proliferation of text-based advertising. Depending on how the system is designed and priced, audience members can compete with large companies for the same ad space.

Kuroshin's community text ads offers a key twist - any community member can publicly comment on an advertisement. "The idea behind ad comments is twofold," explains Foster, Kuroshin's founder. "For the advertiser, the benefit is that potential customers can meet you on 'neutral ground,' ask questions and get more information in a place they're already comfortable. And for the users, the benefit is that they can see what others have said abut the product, whether it's good or bad, and how the advertiser has dealt with other people."

Knowledge management

Some people are taking weblogs and using them as a tool for personal and corporate knowledge management, in what's become known as "klogging." Weblogs have proven to be a great enabler of knowledge collecting and sharing. A strong emphasis on hypertext linking, simple content publishing and syndication helps creators amass a searchable and distributable knowledge base related to personal interests, academic research or the workplace.

Weblogging also encourages interaction and refinement of ideas, enabling a group of peers to add to the knowledge through feedback or comment. Group weblogging has become an effective tool for knowledge management in the workplace. The authors of We Blog: Publishing Online with Weblogs explain one scenario of how weblogs build and capture knowledge: "By integrating the weblog publishing process into how inter-office communication happens, it becomes possible for weblogs to function simultaneously as informal knowledge management systems.

An e-mail exchange between two technical support reps outlining a fix to a common problem can be copied to the department weblog. Now that fix, that knowledge, is stored in a centralized location, and is available to everyone else in the group." .

In the future, online news would give readers the ability to choose only the topics and sources that interested them. To actively allow a reader to narrow the scope of coverage, observed some, could undermine the "philosophical underpinnings of traditional media."The vision that seemed cutting edge and worrisome eight years ago seems to have come partly true. Millions of Yahoo members customize their MyYahoo personal news portal with the same news wire reports that editors use in daily newspapers across the globe. Google's news page uses a computer algorithm to select headlines from thousands of news sites - creating a global newsstand, of sorts.

And media outlets from Fox News and the Drudge Report to individual weblogs offer the kind of opinionated slant to the news that Nicholas Negroponte envisioned. But is the future of online news simply a continued extrapolation of this trend - news a la carte? Does greater personalization necessarily mean greater understanding for a democracy? In the view of futurist and author Watts Wacker, the question is not about greater personalization but about greater perspectives. According to Wacker, the world is moving faster than people can keep up with it. As a result, there are fewer common cultural references that can be agreed upon. Ideas, styles, products and mores accelerate their way from the fringe to the mainstream with increasing speed.

To combat the confusion, consumers are seeking more perspectives, Wacker says. They research an automobile for purchase by spending time online and reading both professional and amateur reviews alike. But what are they doing when it comes to news? And what will they be doing in the future? To understand that, Wacker advises, you must seek out people from the future today and study them.How do you find people from the future? Locate early adopters - people who are using and appropriating technology in new ways.

In South Korea, it looks like one future of online news has arrived a few years early. OhmyNews.com is the most influential online news site in that country, attracting an estimated 2 million readers a day. What's unusual about OhmyNews.com is that readers not only can pick and choose the news they want to read - they also write it. With the help of more than 26,000 registered citizen journalists, this collaborative online newspaper has emerged as a direct challenge to established media outlets in just four years.Unlike its competitors, OhmyNews has embraced the speed, responsiveness and community- oriented nature of the Web.

Rise of "We Media"

The venerable profession of journalism finds itself at a rare moment in history where, for the first time, its hegemony as gatekeeper of the news is threatened by not just new technology and competitors but, potentially, by the audience it serves. Armed with easy-to-use Web publishing tools, always-on connections and increasingly powerful mobile devices, the online audience has the means to become an active participant in the creation and dissemination of news and information. And it's doing just that on the Internet:

1. According to the Pew Internet Project, the terrorist attacks of Sept. 11, 2001, generated the most traffic to traditional news sites in the history of the Web. Many large news sites buckled under the immense demand and people turned to e-mail, weblogs and forums "as conduits for information, commentary, and action related to 9/11 events."The response on the Internet gave rise to a new proliferation of "do-it-yourself journalism." Everything from eyewitness accounts and photo galleries to commentary and personal storytelling emerged to help people collectively grasp the confusion, anger and loss felt in the wake of the tragedy.

During the first few days of the war in Iraq, Pew found that 17 percent of online Americans used the Internet as their principal source of information about the war, a level more than five times greater than those who got their news online immediately after the Sept. 11 terrorist attacks (3 percent). The report also noted that "weblogs (were) gaining a following among a small number of Internet users (4 percent)."

— Immediately after the Columbia shuttle disaster, news and government organizations, in particular The Dallas Morning News and NASA, called upon the public to submit eyewitness accounts and photographs that might lead to clues to the cause of the spacecraft's disintegration.

— ABCNews.com's The Note covers 2004 political candidates and gives each an individual weblog to comment back on what was reported.In addition, presidential candidate Howard Dean guest-blogged on Larry Lessig's weblog for a week in July 2003. (A future president of the United States might be chosen not only on his or her merits, charisma, experience or voting record but on the basis of how well he or she blogs.)

— College coaches, players and sports media outlets keep constant vigil on numerous fan forum sites, which have been credited with everything from breaking and making news to rumor-mongering. "You can't go anywhere or do anything and expect not to be seen, because everyone is a reporter now," says Steve Patterson, who operates ugasports.com, a Web site devoted to University of Georgia sports. —Before the Iraq war, the BBC knew it couldn't possibly deploy enough photojournalists to cover the millions of people worldwide who marched in anti-war demonstrations.

Reaching out to its audience, the BBC News asked readers to send in images taken with digital cameras and cell phones with built-in cameras, and it published the best ones on its Web site.Weblogs come of age The Internet, as a medium for news, is maturing. With every major news event, online media evolve. And while news sites have become more responsive and better able to handle the growing demands of readers and viewers, online communities and personal news and information sites are participating in an increasingly diverse and important role that, until recently, has operated without significant notice from mainstream media.

While there are many ways that the audience is now participating in the journalistic process, weblogs have received the most attention from mainstream media in the past year. Weblogs, or blogs as they are commonly known, are the most active and surprising form of this participation. These personal publishing systems have given rise to a phenomenon that shows the markings of a revolution - giving anyone with the right talent and energy the ability to be heard far and wide on the Web.

Weblogs are frequently updated online journals, with reverse-chronological entries and numerous links, that provide up-to-the-minute takes on the writer's life, the news, or on a specific subject of interest. Often riddled with opinionated commentary, they can be personally revealing (such as a college student's ruminations on dorm life) or straightforward and fairly objective (Romenesko). The growth of weblogs has been largely fueled by greater access to bandwidth and low-cost, often free software. These simple easy-to-use tools have enabled new kinds of collaboration unrestricted by time or geography.

The result is an advance of new social patterns and means for self-expression. Blog-like communities like Slashdot.org have allowed a multitude of voices to participate while managing a social order and providing a useful filter on discussion. Weblogs have expanded their influence by attracting larger circles of readers while at the same time appealing to more targeted audiences.

Blogs are in some ways a new form of journalism, open to anyone who can establish and maintain a Web site, and they have exploded in the past year. Mossberg's description of weblogs as a new kind of journalism might trouble established, traditionally trained journalists. But it is a journalism of a different sort, one not tightly confined by the traditions and standards adhered to by the traditional profession.

These acts of citizen engaging in journalism are not just limited to weblogs. They can be found in newsgroups, forums, chat rooms, collaborative publishing systems and peer-to-peer applications like instant messaging. As new forms of participation have emerged through new technologies, many have struggled to name them. As a default, the name is usually borrowed from the enabling technology (i.e., weblogging, forums and usenets).

The term we use - participatory journalism is meant to describe the content and the intent of online communication that often occurs in collaborative and social media. Here's the working definition that we have adopted: Participatory journalism: The act of a citizen, or group of citizens, playing an active role in the process of collecting, reporting, analyzing and disseminating news and information. The intent of this participation is to provide independent, reliable, accurate, wide-ranging and relevant information that a democracy requires.

Participatory journalism is a bottom-up, emergent phenomenon in which there is little or no editorial oversight or formal journalistic work- flow dictating the decisions of a staff. Instead, it is the result of many simultaneous, distributed conversations that either blossom or quickly atrophy in the Web's social network. While the explosion of weblogs is a recent phenomenon, the idea of tapping into your audience for new perspectives or turning readers into reporters or commentators is not.

Many news organizations have a long history of tapping into their communities and experimenting with turning readers into reporters or commentators. In the early 1990s, newspapers experimented with the idea of civic journalism, which sought participation from readers and communities in the form of focus groups, polls and reaction to daily news stories. Most of these early projects centered around election coverage. Later, newspapers sought to involve communities in major deliberations on public problems such as race, development and crime.

At least 20 percent of the 1,500 daily U.S. newspapers practiced some form of civic journalism between 1994 and 2001. Nearly all said it had a positive effect on the community. Civic journalism has a somewhat controversial reputation, and not everyone is convinced of its benefits. While civic journalism actively tries to encourage participation, the news organization maintains a high degree of control by setting the agenda, choosing the participants and moderating the conversation. Some feel that civic journalism is often too broad, focusing on large issues such as crime and politics, and not highly responsive to the day-to-day needs of the audience.Yet, the seed from which civic journalism grows is dialogue and conversation.

Similarly, a defining characteristic of participatory journalism is conversation. However, there is no central news organization controlling the exchange of information. Conversation is the mechanism that turns the tables on the traditional roles of journalism and creates a dynamic, egalitarian give-and-take ethic. The fluidity of this approach puts more emphasis on the publishing of information rather than the filtering. Conversations happen in the community for all to see.

In contrast, traditional news organizations are set up to filter information before they publish it. It might be collaborative among the editors and reporters, but the debates are not open to public scrutiny or involvement. In an era when anyone can be a reporter or commentator on the Web, 'you move to a two-way journalism.' The journalist becomes a 'forum leader,' or a mediator rather than simply a teacher or lecturer. The audience becomes not consumers, but 'pro-sumers,' a hybrid of consumer and producer. Participatory journalism does not show evidence of needing a classically trained "journalist" to be the mediator or facilitator.

Plenty of weblogs, forums and online communities appear to function effectively without one. This raises some important questions: If par-ticipatory journalism has risen without the direct help of trained journalists or news industry initiatives, what role will mainstream media play? And are mainstream media willing to relinquish some control and actively collaborate with their audiences? Or will an informed and empowered consumer begin to frame the news agenda from the grassroots? And, will journalism's values endure?

The new interactive medium both threatens the status quo and promises an exciting new way of learning about the world. This deftly describes both camps of opinion concerning participation by the audience in journalism. It's not just the Internet that threatens the status quo of the news business. Now we can say that the news business is undergoing "a momentous transition."

According to the authors, each time there has been a period of significant, social, economic and technological change, a transformation in news occurred. This happened in the 1830s-40s with the advent of the telegraph; the 1880s with a drop in paper prices and a wave of immigration; the 1920s with radio and the rise of gossip and celebrity culture; the 1950s at the onset of the Cold War and television.

The arrival of cable, followed by the Internet and mobile technologies, has brought the latest upheaval in news. And this time, the change in news may be even more dramatic. For the first time in our history, the news increasingly is produced by companies outside journalism, and this new economic organization is important. We are facing the possibility that independent news will be replaced by self-interested commercialism posing as news. New technology, along with globalization and the conglomeration of media, is causing a shift away from journalism that is connected to citizen building and one that supports a healthy democracy.

Clearly, journalism is in the process of redefining itself, adjusting to the disruptive forces surrounding it. So it's no surprise that discussions about forms of participatory journalism, such as weblogs, are frequently consumed by defensive debates about what is journalism and who can legitimately call themselves a journalist. While debating what makes for good journalism is worthwhile, and is clearly needed, it prevents the discussion from advancing to any analysis about the greater good that can be gained from audience participation in news.

Furthermore, the debate often exacerbates the differences primarily in processes, overlooking obvious similarities. If we take a closer look at the basic tasks and values of traditional journalism, the differences become less striking. From a task perspective, journalism is seen as "the profession of gathering, editing, and publishing news reports and related articles for newspapers, magazines, television, or radio."In terms of journalism's key values, there is much debate. The primary purpose of journalism is to provide citizens with the information they need to be free and self-governing.

In the case of the aforementioned South Korean news site, we see that traditional journalism's basic tasks and values are central to its ethos. The difference essentially boils down to a redistribution of control - a democratization of media. "With OhmyNews, we wanted to say goodbye to 20th-century journalism where people only saw things through the eyes of the mainstream, conservative media," said Oh Yeon-ho, editor and founder of South Korea's Ohmynews.com."The main concept is that every citizen can be a reporter," Yeon-ho says. "A reporter is the one who has the news and who is trying to inform others."

The new evolving media ecosystem The most obvious difference between participatory journalism and traditional journalism is the different structure and organization that produce them. Traditional media are created by hierarchical organizations that are built for commerce. Their business models are broadcast and advertising focused. They value rigorous editorial workflow, profitability and integrity. Participatory journalism is created by networked communities that value conversation, collaboration and egalitarianism over profitability.

The order of things in broadcast is 'filter, then publish.' The order in communities is 'publish, then filter.' If you go to a dinner party, you don't submit your potential comments to the hosts, so that they can tell you which ones are good enough to air before the group, but this is how broadcast works every day. Writers submit their stories in advance, to be edited or rejected before the public ever sees them. Participants in a community, by contrast, say what they have to say, and the good is sorted from the mediocre after the fact.

Many traditional journalists are dismissive of participatory journalism, particularly webloggers, characterizing them as self-interested or unskilled amateurs. Conversely, many webloggers look upon mainstream media as an arrogant, exclusive club that puts its own version of self-interest and economic survival above the societal responsibility of a free press. According to Shirky, what the mainstream media fail to understand is that despite a participant's lack of skill or journalistic training, the Internet itself acts as editing mechanism, with the difference that "editorial judgment is applied at the edges ... after the fact, not in advance."

This kind of high-tech interaction is a journalism that resembles conversation again, much like the original journalism occurring in the publick houses and coffeehouses four hundred years ago. Seen in this light, journalism's function is not fundamentally changed by the digital age. The techniques may be different, but the underlying principles are the same. What is emerging is a new media ecosystem, where online communities discuss and extend the stories created by mainstream media. These communities also produce participatory journalism, grassroots reporting, annotative reporting, commentary and factchecking, which the mainstream media feed upon, developing them as a pool of tips, sources and story ideas.

Weblogs expand the media universe. They are a media life-form that is native to the Web, and they add something new to our mix, something valuable, something that couldn't have existed before the Web. "It should be obvious that weblogs aren't competing with the work of the professional journalism establishment, but rather complementing it. If the pros are criticized as being cautious, impersonal, corporate and herdlike, the bloggers are the opposite in, well, almost every respect: They're reckless, confessional, funky - and herdlike.

Behind the Explosion of Participatory Media

Newspapermen of the Victorian era feared the telegraph would spell their doom. "The mere newspapers must submit to destiny and go out of existence," wrote one newspaper executive. Yet, just the opposite occurred. Despite fears of their obsolescence, newspapers were able to thwart a major technological threat by adopting it as a business advantage. The telegraph was speedier than mail and enabled newspapers to publish more timely news. Other newspapers joined together to set up wire services such as the Associated Press. And the concern that a telegraph transmission might be cut short gave rise to the familiar writing style called the inverted pyramid, which places important news first followed by less critical details.

Journalism has always had to respond to technological and social changes. The Information Age brought about a tremendous expansion of media - cable television, growing numbers of niche print publications, Internet Web sites, mobile telephony. Media have become nearly ubiquitous, and journalism again finds itself at a crossroads as the media landscape becomes more fragmented and filled with competition from nontraditional sources.

"The way we get news has gone through momentous transition," Kovach and Rosenstiel write in The Elements of Journalism. "It has happened each time there is a period of significant social, economic and technological change. It is occurring now with the advent of cable followed by the Internet. The collision this time may be more dramatic." Unlike the telegraph, the Internet is far more pervasive and accessible by just about anyone. If history is any guide, journalism will change, although how dramatic that change will be remains uncertain.

Social Networks

People are inherently social creatures. We develop and maintain complex social networks of friends, family and acquaintances through various means of communication. Regardless of technology, human "relationships will naturally continue to rely on face-to-face and physical contact, on shared experience and values, on acts of generosity and thoughtfulness, and on trust, understanding and empathy," according to a whitepaper for Groove, the collaboration software created by Lotus developer Ray Ozzie.

"Nevertheless, (Internet and mobile) technologies do have the potential to have significant, fundamental impact on the types of relationships we maintain, on where we live and work, on when and how we are educated, on how we entertain ourselves and spend our leisure time, on our politics, and on how we conceive of time." In the 10 years since its mass adoption, the Web has quickly become a reflection of our elaborate social networks. It has evolved into a powerful medium for communication and collaboration, as evidenced by the hypertext links of more than 10 billion documents authored by millions of people and organizations around the world.

It is the greatest publishing system ever known, and it keeps growing. In May 2003, there were at least 40.4 million Web sites with thousands being added, moved or removed every day. It's a phenomenally extraordinary achievement, which has emerged without central planning and without government regulation, censor or sanction - an emergent, bottom-up process. Self-organization is an irrepressible human drive, and the Internet is a toolkit for self-organizing. The role of voluntary cooperation is the most important and least known story in the history of personal computers and networks.

Indeed, the architecture of the Internet was the result of a decentralized philosophy, free software and collaboration. In 1962, Paul Baran of the RAND corporation was commissioned by the U.S. Air Force to design a computer network able to survive a nuclear attack to any part of it. His insightful solution required that there be no master or central computer running the network. Instead, computers could be connected to many other computers in a mesh-like pattern. In a sense, Baran wanted to create a social network of mainframes that routed packets of information through a variable maze of connectors. The benefit was that the network could grow, or handle a loss of computers, without having to be redesigned.

As brilliant as Baran's idea was, it was rejected. AT&T, the telephone monopoly designated to maintain the network for the U.S. government, saw the "digital packet" approach as too costly to deploy and a threat to its monopoly position because it could allow for competition.

But several years later, the Advanced Research Project Agency stumbled upon the same solution and created a network called ARPANET, the precursor to today's Internet. The network was built to allow military facilities to connect computers. By 1973, just three years after ARPANET went online, something unexpected happened. E-mail, which began as a novelty, accounted for 75 percent of all network traffic.

Throughout the 1980s, the Internet grew steadily but remained mostly unnoticed behind the walls of academic and scientific institutions. In the early '90s, two events turned the Internet into the greatest publishing system in history by making it more accessible to the masses. First, Tim Berners-Lee, a researcher at CERN, substituted the impossible-to-remember numerical addressing system of the Internet with the URL (uniform resource locator) for use as electronic addresses. Soon after, students at the University of Illinois, led by Marc Andreessen, created Mosaic, the first browser to display documents on the Web. This graphic, rather than text-based, interface resulted in an explosion of the Internet's popularity.

In December 1993, a New York Times business section article concluded that Mosaic was perhaps "an application program so different and so obviously useful that it can create a new industry from scratch." Years before the advent of the Web and Mosaic, email, bulletin boards and Usenet were the popular means of communication and collaboration on the Internet. Bulletin boards and Usenet, a stockpile of millions of email postings arranged into "newsgroups," changed radically and became more popular as forums. The browser-based graphic interface, which allowed participants to explore and contribute more readily, changed the practical nature of the Usenet idea into something more open, accessible and interesting to the masses.

The Internet had become a massive repository of publicly accessible, linked documents. This doesn't sound like a breeding ground for social activity, but according to John Seely Brown and Paul Duguid, it is inherently so. "Documents do not merely carry information, they help make it, structure it and validate it. More intriguing, perhaps, documents also help structure society, enabling social groups to form, develop, and maintain a sense of shared identity," they write in The Social Life of Information. "Shared and circulating documents, it seems, have long provided interesting social glue."

Today, we see a new phenomenon. Given technological innovations in open source software, everyone has access to robust tools for publishing and collaborating easily on the Web. Weblogging tools are in many ways easier to use than most e-mail applications. It is this ease that accounts for their increasing popularity. Estimates of the number of active weblogs vary widely from 500,000 to as high as 1 million. According to the Pew Internet & American Life Project, more than 8 million U.S. Internet users (7 percent) have created a weblog and 90 million (84 percent) have participated in online groups.

Post-Information Age

In a way, the Internet was destined to be a social medium from the start - open, unregulated, extensible and unpredictable. Like the telephone, it removes one of the critical barriers to maintaining social networks: geography. In doing so, the Internet enables a vibrant social universe to emerge powered by the passions of millions. Moreover, this medium has empowered millions to express their ideas and perspectives in many ways, which, according to futurist Watts Wacker, feeds a great hunger in the Post-Information Age.

In his 2002 book The Deviant's Advantage, Wacker suggests that our current society is undergoing relentless, all-encompassing change, which will do nothing but accelerate. This constant change results in an "Abolition of Context" - the inability of business and society to find commonly agreed upon reference points. "Context is the framework, the structure, the collective common understanding that allows us to live our lives and run our businesses," Wacker writes in his book. "Take it away and it's all but impossible to know what's the right or wrong action to take."

Such a situation makes it more difficult for companies to create commercially viable, long-lasting goods and services. This environment also creates stress, anxiety and confusion for the individual. With social mores constantly shifting, people seek a "proliferation of perspectives" to make sense of the world. Credibility, a traditionally reliable context as it has been viewed until now, is dead, Wacker says. "Knowing what other people think news means, in many layers, is more important."

It appears that the many forms of participatory journalism on the Web are ideally suited to serve this function. There is evidence that people are actively seeking new perspectives beyond those provided by mainstream media. Researchers have begun to categorize an individual's media diet as a more dependable method of segmenting audiences, as opposed to demographic and psychographic criteria. We are now beginning to lead what futurist Wacker calls "media-centric life," where all of our information is mediated, coming to us second or third hand. Media, he says, are how we define ourselves and our relationships.

This media-centric life requires a large amount of assimilation of information, most of it coming second-hand. Objectivity is one casualty of this massive abundance of viewpoints, Wacker argues. Even traditionalists are questioning the practicality of objectivity. In The Elements of Journalism, Kovach and Rosenstiel write: "The concept of objectivity is so mangled it now is usually used to describe the very problem it was conceived to correct." But whether the demise of objectivity will give rise to a social environment governed by interests and relationships is debatable. What is clear is that the Internet provides more opportunity for people to share information among communities, thereby circumventing traditional media's role as privileged, trusted and informed intermediaries of the news.

In their report "Online Communities: Networks that nurture long-distance relationships and local ties," the Pew Internet & American Life Project found that not only are people becoming more social online, they are forming vibrant communities and integrating them into their lives. Some of their findings:

— 90 million Americans (84 percent of Internet users) have participated in online groups; 26 percent have used the Internet to deepen their ties to their local communities.

— Use of the Internet often prompts Americans to join groups. More than half of the aforementioned 90 million say they joined an online group after they began participating over the Internet.

— Online communities bring about greater contact with different people. Participants say that online communities have spurred connections to strangers and to people of different racial, ethnic and economic backgrounds.

— Online communities foster lively chatter and connection. People exchange emails, hash out issues, find out about group activities, and meet face to face as a result of online communities. About 23 million Americans are very active in online communities, meaning that they email their principal online group several times a week.

— Online communities draw civic involvement from the young, a segment of the population that has not typically been drawn to civic activities.

Sociologist Barry Wellman argues that many new social arrangements are being formed through "glocalization" - the capacity of the Internet to expand people's social worlds to faraway people and simultaneously connect them more deeply to the place they live. More than just connecting, people are increasingly collaborating. The bottom-up nature of the Internet and several technological innovations - such as digital still and video cameras, mobile devices and wireless computing platforms - have resulted in an explosion of creative activity.

Just as weblogs and forums have turned audiences into participants, other industries have thrived by developing tools to turn their customers into creators. As Stefan Thomke and Eric von Hippel argue in "Customers as Innovators: A New Way to Create Value," the pace of change in many markets is too great and "the cost of understanding and responding to customers' needs can quickly spiral out of control." Some industries have already succeeded in turning their customers into contributors and innovators. Knowing they cannot predict the shifting desires of their customers, these companies have instead created the tools and frameworks to empower their customers to create.

"Essentially, these companies have abandoned their efforts to understand exactly what products their customers want and have instead equipped them with tools to design and develop their own products, ranging from minor modifications to major new innovations," Thomke and von Hippel wrote. A number of industries are succeeding in the "Customer as Innovator" approach. Nestle has built a toolkit that enables its customers to develop their own flavors. GE provides customers with Web-based tools for designing better plastic products. This approach has transformed the semiconductor business, bringing the custom-chip market to more than $15 billion.

Providing the tools and services to enable customers to act as their own auctioneers is at the heart of one of the most successful Internet companies, eBay. In 2002, eBay members bought and sold $14.87 billion in annualized gross merchandise. Perhaps one the most vivid and dramatic examples of customers transforming a business is the computer game industry. Many of the best game companies now count on modders to show them the way creatively and to ensure their own survival in a savagely competitive market. By fostering the creativity of their fans, their more agile peers in the game industry have not only survived but prospered.

In many ways, the open-source movement offers a glimpse at the future. In open-source projects, the community builds the tools for itself motivated by hopes of creating better software through mass collaboration. In the best case, open-source movements can organize and develop industry-leading tools (e.g., Linux and Apache Web server), which sometimes threaten multibillion-dollar companies.

According to Dave Winer, weblog guru and founder of Userland Software, Google's acquisition of Pyra and its Blogger weblogging tool earlier this year "may signal a change possibly as deep as the personal computer revolution, where huge glass palaces controlled by technologists were routed around, by software and hardware that did the same thing, for a fraction of the cost. Today, the same software that Vignette sold a few years ago for millions of dollars can be had for hundreds, and it's much easier to install and use." Access to powerful and inexpensive tools is turning more people into innovators of all sorts. The challenge for news organizations, ultimately, will be to persuade their customers to become not just innovators but collaborators as well.

Power of Networks

In their book *Information Rules*, Carl Shapiro and Hal R. Varian suggest an altogether new axiom for the news business and its future. "The old industrial economy was driven by economies of scale; the new information economy is driven by the economics of networks." Indeed, our traditional notions of economics are being disrupted and transformed by the power of distributed collaboration through our computer networks. More than 2 million people worldwide have been donating their unused computer down time to help the Search for Extraterrestrial Intelligence (SETI) analyze 50 billions bytes of signals from outer space. The SETI@home project, which began in mid-1999, put distributed computing on the map.

About the same time that project began, the peer-to-peer file sharing program Napster was launched to enable the sharing of music between users connected to the Internet. At its height, 70 million users were trading 2.7 billion files per month. Since Napster was shut down, Gnutella clients such as Morpheus and Kazaa have stepped in, allowing billions of movies, songs, ebooks, software and other digital files to be exchanged among the masses.

It seems as though the possibilities of distributed collaboration are limitless. "Today, millions of people and their PCs are not just looking for messages from outer space and trading music," says Rheingold in Smart Mobs, "but tackling cancer research, finding prime numbers, rendering films, forecasting weather, designing synthetic drugs by running simulations on billions of possible molecules - taking on computing problems so massive that scientists have not heretofore considered them." The network economy and the proliferation of media are presenting a tremendous challenge for mainstream media organizations, such as newspapers, radio and television. Not only will they have to adapt organizationally, and perhaps philosophically, but their products, over time, will be transformed in unexpected and unforeseen ways.

7

Implications of Media in Public Relations

The abundance and proliferation of virtual communities and collaboration environments provide the opportunity for anyone to play just about any role in the journalistic process. For media organizations and businesses to understand how to engage their empowered audience, we must consider what motivates the audience to take on their new roles and what kinds of rules yield the most fruitful participation. Finally, we look at reputation systems and the balance of trust that's struck between buyers and sellers or content creators and their online peers.

Media Sources

Through these emerging electronic communities, the Web has enabled its users to create, increase or renew their social capital. These communities are not merely trading grounds for information but a powerful extension of our social networks. And as in any social system, looking at our motivations helps us understand and trust the system as well as find our place in it. The Hierarchy of Needs was the brainchild of Abraham Maslow, one of the founding fathers of humanistic psychology. He believed that people are motivated by the urge to satisfy needs ranging from basic survival to self-fulfillment, and that they don't fill the higher-level needs until the lower-level ones are satisfied.

Social recognition is one of the biggest motivators, intoxicating participants with instant gratification and approval. This ego-driven motivation to enhance social capital is best captured by the advice Web sites and review engines rampant in the late 1990s, which enabled anyone to showcase his or her expertise and recommendations on just about any subject imaginable. "People with expertise contributed answers, tidbits, essays, pages of software code, lore of astonishing variety," Howard Rheingold writes in Smart Mobs. "A few contributors earned the kind of currency banks accept. Most contributed for the social recognition that came with being a top-ranked reviewer. The 'reputation managers' that enabled users and other recommenders to rate each other made possible opinion markets that traded almost entirely on ego gratification."

For some, the ego-driven surface of this motivation is more practical underneath - people want to establish themselves as an authority on a subject. For example, one the primary reasons people write a blog is that they aspire to become "legitimate" writers in mainstream media. The weblog becomes a place to hone their craft and showcase their skills. In general, this is viewed as a benefit to the individual.

Small business proprietors, consultants and budding writers can quickly gain an audience and build a positive reputation that they can parlay into real-world business opportunities. But organizations can benefit as well because individual reputation can be transferred to some extent. For example, if a reporter begins to gain an involved audience through a weblog, that good will and trust could be transferred to the media organization that he or she works for. These new forms also allow people who haven't had a voice - because of educational, economic, social or cultural barriers - to enter the dialogue by building a personal reputation. Online communities have also empowered those with physical or emotional impediments to blossom in a virtual space.

To create connections with others who have similar interests, online and off. An oft-read claim is that the majority of the billions of Web pages on the Internet today are junk. The trouble with this criticism is that the wheat - the relevant 2 percent - is different for every person. What many dismiss as "junk" is made by junkies - people who are fanatical or passionate about a subject. People want to feed their obsessions and share them with like-minded individuals. This is what fuels, in large part, many social connections on the Internet. Whether it's a fan page for '50s and '60s jazz pianist and vocalist Buddy Greco, or a database of airfoils used in the wing design of aircraft, people are using online communities to share passions, beliefs, hobbies and lifestyles.

According to a study by the Pew Internet & American Life Project, about 45 million participants in online communities say the Internet has "helped them connect with groups or people who share their interests." Participation in an online community, the study says, has helped them get to know people they otherwise would not have met. The same Pew study revealed that these virtual relationships are transferring to offline interaction. "In addition to helping users participate in communities of interest that often have no geographical boundaries, the Internet is a tool for those who are involved with local groups, particularly church groups (28 million). Internet users have employed the Internet to contact or get information about local groups."

Sociologist Barry Wellman argues that a good deal of new social capital is being formed through "glocalization" - the capacity of the Internet to expand users' social worlds to faraway people and simultaneously to connect them more deeply to the place where they live. According to the Pew study, "glocalization" is widespread. "The Internet helps many people find others who share their interests no matter how distant they are, and it also helps them increase their contact with groups and people they already know and it helps them feel more connected to them."

Sense-making and Understanding

Faced with an overwhelming flow of information from a massive number of media sources, people are increasingly going to online communities to learn how to make sense of things. Moreover, the conglomeration and corporatization of media and the sophisticated means by which sources (such as politicians and business executives) "spin" media leaves the mass audience often grasping to make sense of the news and wondering what information to trust.

Witness the increasing number of experts on TV news trying to explain market fluctuations, political maneuvers and medical advancements. But that doesn't completely satisfy the audience, write Bill Kovach and Tom Rosenstiel in their book The Elements of Journalism, because "a journalism that focuses on the expert elite - the special interests - may be in part responsible for public disillusionment. Such a press does not reflect the world as most people live and experience it."

Weblogs, forums, usenets and other online social forms have become real-time wellsprings of sense-making from their peers on just about any subject. They also function as archives of perspective. According to a study by the Pew Internet & American Life Project, "The pull of online communities in the aftermath of the September 11 attacks shows how Americans have integrated online communities into their lives. In the days following the attacks, 33 percent of American Internet users read or posted material in chat rooms, bulletin boards, or other online forums. Although many early posts reflected outrage at the events, online discussions soon migrated to grieving, discussion and debate on how to respond, and information queries about the suspects and those who sponsored them."

To inform and be informed

Participants in discussion forums, weblogs and collaborative publishing communities also play the role of "thin media" publishers, inexpensively providing news, information and advice not normally found in mainstream media. Everyone on the Internet is a potential expert on some subject - from Pez dispensers to digital photography techniques to wormholes - and these participatory forms are great places to find and share not only obscure or rare information, but commentary that might be too controversial for mainstream media.

"Thin media publishers are far nimbler and will feed happily on new niches that are far too obscure for traditional media to notice and too thin for traditional media to profitably mine," says Henry Copeland, founder of the Web consultancy Pressflex and author of the weblog Blogads. "And, because they are small and nimble, thin media can help discover and invent the Next Big Thing much easier than their big peers who are busy looking for huge revenues from huge services." The social network created by Internet virally spreads information extremely quickly among their participants. This may be because participatory forms attract "mavens" and "connectors."

Mavens are information brokers, sharing and trading what they know. They are aggressive collectors of information but are socially motivated to share it as well. Connectors are people who know a lot of people in diverse settings. They have their feet in many different worlds and are socially motivated to bring them together. Participatory forms offer an excellent outlet for mavens to satisfy their need to share and acquire information, and provides connectors the ability to help information seekers find mavens. (It also provides the opportunity to position themselves as an authority on a subject.)

In a foreword to Seth Godin's book on marketing, Unleashing the Ideavirus, Gladwell explains the potential power of what's happening in participatory forms: "(The) most successful ideas are those that spread and grow because of the customer's relationship to other customers - not the marketer's to the customer." Later in the book, Godin adds: "The future belongs to marketers who establish a foundation and process where interested people can market to each other. Ignite consumer networks and then get out of the way and let them talk."

To entertain and be entertained

Just about anything will suffice as entertainment, as long as it can serve as a distraction from the day-to-day grind. To get people to pay for this diversion, it usually must be compelling or "fun." And there are seemingly no limits to what we will pay for fun. But, as anyone in the entertainment business will testify, fun can be one of the most difficult experiences to satisfy. What seems to resonate with an audience of thousands one month falls into relative obscurity the next month. Factors such as novelty, trend and cultural status weigh heavily in the success of entertainment. The result is a large target that is hard to hit.

The Web is not a natural vehicle for prepackaged entertainment. Unlike the lockstep conformity imposed by television, advertising and corporate propaganda, the Net has given new legitimacy - and freedom - to play. Many of those drawn into this world find themselves exploring a freedom never before imagined: to indulge their curiosity, to debate, to disagree, to laugh at themselves, to compare visions, to learn, to create new art, new knowledge.

Online participation is simply fun - whether a political riff by a deeply committed weblogger, a casual forum discussion, or a one-off album review posted on Amazon. As futurist Paul Saffo notes, "In the end, much of what passes for communications actually has a high entertainment component. The most powerful hybrid of communications and entertainment is 'particitainment' - entertaining communications that connects us with some larger purpose or enterprise."

Those who participate online usually create content to inform and entertain others. But creating also builds self-esteem and, in Maslow's view, it's an act of self-actualization. We derive fulfillment from the act of creation. "Five percent of the populace (probably even less) can create. The others watch, listen, read, consume," says Marc Canter, one of the founders of Macromedia and now chairman and founder of Broadband Mechanics. "I think one of the destinies of digital technology is to enable the other 95 percent to express their creativity somehow. That's the gestalt view."

"Digital cameras, storytelling, assembling stuff from existing content, annotating, reviews, conversations, linking topics together - are all forms of creativity," Canter says. "(Weblogging is) at the core of creativity - expressing your feelings, opinions and showing everyone else what you think is important." Traditional media tend to understate the value of participation journalism, holding that comments, reviews and content created by "amateurs" provide little value to their mass audience. As such, they are missing the inherent psychological value of the creative process to the individual.

For the most part, our list contains motivations that are positive or fairly benign. An egalitarian/for-the-common-good ethic tends to permeate most of these forms. Yet, anyone that has participated in online communities knows that not all participants play fairly. People will abuse these forms by performing pranks, manipulating the rules, spreading false information and rumors, engaging in flaming - indeed, just about any mischief imaginable - and the results can serious.

According to a CNET article in 1996, "Several stocks have seen meteoric rises, or dramatic falls, in their valuation because of information posted to Internet newsgroups and online services. The Securities and Exchange Commission and other federal regulatory agencies are concerned that unscrupulous insiders or stock promoters could disseminate false or misleading information to manipulate securities prices." Regulatory agencies have policed Internet postings aimed at manipulating stock prices, but they need to tread carefully lest they infringe on free speech rights.

Conflict is a key component of any social environment, from a party to a chat room, so we have learned to develop rules designed to guide the experience in a positive direction. "Social interaction creates tension between the individual and the group," explains Clay Shirky, a consultant and teacher who writes frequently on the social and economic effects of Internet technologies. "This is true of all social interaction, not just online. Any system that supports groups addresses this tension by enacting a simple constitution - a set of rules governing the relationship between individuals and the groups. These constitutions usually work by encouraging or requiring certain kinds of interaction, and discouraging or forbidding others."

In broadcast models, the rules of participation are strict and limited. The media organization has supreme control as the informed intermediary of the news and it only allows the audience to participate through limited means, e.g., submitting letters to the editor or phoning a talk show. Mainstream media are comfortable with this level of participation because it's relatively easy to authenticate the credibility of these participants (though occasional pranks do occur).

Because not all participatory journalism is collaborative, We Media can follow the same model as broadcast models. For example, reviews are submitted by the audience to a product recommendation site, authenticated by editors, and broadcast out to a mass audience. Likewise, many webloggers have little interaction or open discussion with their audience. It's simply push media. But collaborative forms of participatory journalism - forums, newsgroups, chat rooms, group weblogs and publishing systems - are more complex because they must balance the tension between the group and the individual.

Even more challenging are the dynamically forming groups that come together briefly to achieve goals through Internet-connected mobile devices (dubbed "smart mobs" by

Rheingold). In the past few decades, the Internet has become highly successful in giving the consumer a voice, but author Stephen Johnson says "... systems like Slashdot force us to accept a more radical proposition. To understand how these new media experiences work, you have to analyze the message, the medium and the rules. What's interesting here is not just the medium, but rather the rules that govern what gets selected and what doesn't."

When we talk about rules, we really are describing control - the governance of how participants assume roles, how they are allowed to interact with others, and the ownership of the social system. The rules of participation come from a few places. First, they come from technology - rules that are built into the social software that runs the community or participatory form. These rules are then configured by the host (whoever creates the environment). A basic rule of most systems, for example, is that you have to become a registered member to participate. A host would define whether registration is necessary and the criteria that a registrant must meet.

Second, rules come from the community of members. This can come from moderators - appointed community members who police the ebb and flow of communication based on the established rules of the environment. For example, in chat rooms or discussion forums, it's common to have a moderator that disciplines or kicks out users who are behaving improperly. Even those who are not appointed as moderators will police the activity of the system. Much as in any social situation, individuals draw boundaries about what's appropriate and what's not.

As the community grows and evolves, members push back against the rules of the host to the point where the system becomes co-owned and operated. In this regard, many of these environments are highly democratic in the way they operate. Various technologies have evolved over the past 40 years to enable us to establish rules, monitor behavior and to tune out the unwanted voices. As online community expert Rheingold says, "Hiding the crap is the easy part. The real achievement is finding quality." To increase the signal-to-noise ratio of online communities, emerging technologies called "reputation systems" are helping participants define which information is credible, reliable and trustworthy.

Reputation systems

Traditional models of trust between buyers and sellers fell short of requirements for an online marketplace, where anonymous transactions crossed territorial and legal boundaries as well as traditional value chains. Alternative quantifications of trust were developed for ecommerce, called "reputation systems" or "trust metrics," to ensure better evaluations of risk. On eBay, for example, auction buyers evaluate sellers, rating their transaction experience and adding comments. The cumulative ranking of past buyers creates a track record of trust that new buyers often reference. This also works in the other direction, where sellers can rate buyers, creating a full-circle reputation system.

"A reputation system collects, distributes, and aggregates feedback about participants' past behavior," according to a paper by a group of University of Michigan researchers. "Though few of the producers or consumers of the ratings know each other, these systems help people decide whom to trust, encourage trustworthy behavior, and deter participation by those who are unskilled or dishonest." When it comes to the exchange of news and information, the challenge of reputation systems is equally complex to that of ecommerce. In traditional broadcast models, trust is built top down.

News and information is gathered and disseminated by trained professionals that use rigorous methods of verification to ensure that the information is reliable and trustworthy. The media institution develops a certain level of credibility based on the success of this process. From the consumer's perspective, it's easy to place trust in an established institution such as The Wall Street Journal or even MTV, but how does the audience learn to trust a stranger (or group of strangers), to evaluate the information they are providing, and to collaborate with them?

In participatory forms, trust is built from the bottom up. An anonymous individual enters the environment with no reputation and must gain the trust of others through their behavior and through the information they provide. Through the ranking and rating of content and of content creators, several successful online communities have used reputation systems to help maintain quality discussions and content.

One of the most well-known success stories of reputation systems is Slashdot.org, an online technology discussion community. Slashdot has three mechanisms for creating and distributing trust. First, all posts to the site are policed by moderators, who are members in good standing. Second, moderators are monitored by meta-moderators to ensure that moderators do not wield too much control. The last ingredient is karma, a way for members to gain recognition for contributions and appropriate behavior. "These three political concepts," says Shirky, "lightweight as they are, allow Slashdot to grow without becoming unusable." Reputation systems help track the activity of a community and use criteria to determine appropriate roles for members, based on their level of acceptance within the community.

Reputation systems also help members identify self-interested parties that are trying to disrupt the community's goal of the greater good. According to the creators of Kaitiaki.org, a community site in New Zealand, reputation systems "have the potential to solve the problems of controlling access while preventing gate-keeping or 'capture' of the web site by outsiders. They serve as a filter so that the most valued members of the community are given prominence, while less valued members have a chance to prove themselves before they are given the 'limelight' [enhanced reputation and special privileges]. In this way, the site can avoid spam (unsolicited advertising), abusive discussions and other bad behaviour that plagues some discussion group systems."

Other online communities have reputations systems that try to capture the somewhat transitive nature of trust. The products recommendation site Epinions uses a "web of trust" to mimic the way people share word-of-mouth advice. Their reputation system is based on the premise, "If a friend consistently gives you good advice, you're likely to believe that person's suggestions in the future. You know which preferences you and your friend share. If you both like the same types of films, you're more likely to trust your friend's recommendations on what to see. Such collaborative filtering systems, pioneered by Firefly (since purchased by Microsoft) in the mid-1990s, are now becoming commonplace, bringing the idea of reputation systems to a wide range of content sites, ranging from parental advice to purchases of home theater systems.

There are other ways to assess credibility of content. One of the most effective is through hyperlinks. Acting as a decentralized, distributed reputation system, links act as votes, citations and reference to relevant pages on the Web. Google's PageRank search algorithm uses hyperlinks-as-votes as a method of relevance in the social network of the web. As they explain on their Web site, "PageRank relies on the uniquely democratic nature of the web by using its vast link structure as an indicator of an individual page's value.

In essence, Google interprets a link from page A to page B as a vote, by page A, for page B. But, Google looks at more than the sheer volume of votes, or links a page receives; it also analyzes the page that casts the vote. Votes cast by pages that are themselves 'important' weigh more heavily and help to make other pages 'important.' " Weblogs use a similar system of hyperlinks as votes with something called "blogrolls." A blogroll is a list of links to a weblog author's favorite Web sites, usually sites that are related to the weblog's subject. So if a reader decides they like a certain weblog, they might check out its blogroll as well.

"Rampant cross-linkage isn't a new phenomenon. It's the basic mechanism by which academia has operated for centuries," says Joshua Allen on his weblog Better Living Through Software. Researchers judge the value of published research based upon the number of other works that cite it. Citations in scientific research form 'clusters' of cross-linkage that would suggest citation reciprocity. Groups of people tend to cite one another. Besides reciprocity, there are certainly other reasons that researchers can end up getting sucked into citation clusters. A milder form of reciprocity is mutual admiration. If Dr. Wang cites Dr. Miller five times, Dr. Miller will start to think that Dr. Wang has good judgment.

There are several other qualities of these new online participatory experiences that can breed trust and credibility:

Egalitarian: Collaborative publishing systems like Wiki use open editing rules and version history to promote trust. Because any reader of a Wiki can add their own views or information to a Wiki article, they begin to trust the environment and the collective goal of the common good. "We assume that the world is mostly full of reasonable people," say the creators of Wikipedia, a multi-lingual open-content encyclopedia, "and that collectively they can arrive eventually at a reasonable conclusion, despite the worst efforts of a very few wreckers."

Intimacy: Authenticity comes from the personal nature of discussions in a participatory form. One powerful draw of weblogs and forums is their ability to capture and share first-hand accounts, such as 9/11 terrorists attacks.

Passion: According to Time magazine columnist James Poniewozik, the problem with mainstream media today is a passion deficit. "Many big-media journalists are now cautious, well-paid conformists distant from their audiences and more responsive to urban élites, powerful people and megacorporations - especially the ones they work for." The result, he says, is bland news anchors, magazines that more closely resemble catalogs, timid pack journalism, and celebrity/cult-of-personality coverage overload.

On the flip side of the new media ecosystem, online participatory journalism is fueled by people who fanatically follow and passionately discuss their favorite subjects. Their weblogs and online communities, while perhaps not as professionally produced, are chock full of style, voice and attitude. Passion makes the experience not only compelling and memorable but also credible.

Speed of communication: According to Harvard University professor Karen Stephenson, an influential social network theorist, one easy way to improve the level of trust is simply to increase the speed with which people respond to our communication. When people return e-mails or respond to questions in forums quickly, it sends a signal that we can rely on them because our connection, however distant, is important enough to claim some of their attention.

Compare the experience of leaving a voice-mail message with tech support that gets a response days later to a real-time chat session or user-to-user discussion forums. The faster a satisfactory answer comes, the more likely we are to trust a person or organization. Human beings always keep an internal accounting system of who owes what to whom. Response time is one indicator of the degree of trustworthiness of the individual.

Free market of media: There are three basic rules of behavior that are tied directly to the intrinsic nature of the Internet: No one owns it. Everyone can use it. Anyone can improve it. Likewise, there is practically no barrier to participatory journalism. Just about anyone can start a discussion forum or weblog for relatively little or no money, or participate for free in most public participatory environments. "This is a medium that by definition encourages readers to establish competing media," says publisher Welch. "That's awesome and wonderful." When the audience owns the medium, and owns the power to equitably compete in the same space, the medium and its forms carry a level of trust not found in any other media to date.

Reputations systems are by no means perfect. One problem with online reputation is the lack of portability of virtual identities (and reputations) between systems. For example, if you build a positive seller or buyer reputation on eBay or Slashdot, it cannot be transferred to other virtual environments. (eBay has sued some who have tried to do so.) It's great for the host of the community, such as eBay - some speculate that this aggregation of social capital is the key to their success - but for the individual and for social networks, it's a serious problem. It creates islands of reputation, which are time-consuming to earn.

The issue of identity ownership may be why weblogs cause such a powerful fuss. The participant owns and controls their identity, without the requirement to be known by a different eight-character name in each system. Because a person has control over his own piece of the community landscape (with a weblog), he feels a powerful ownership of his space that's lacking in traditional community sites. (Weblogging) tools are exciting because they point to the future of online community - a future where everyone has a home of his own, a space where he has control, a private space in an ever-more complicated virtual community sphere.

From the reader's perspective, this also adds a level of credibility to webloggers because bloggers typically use their real-world identity in their virtual space. Another challenge facing reputation systems is capturing feedback. Some people may not bother to provide feedback at all, seeing little or no value in the process. Negative feedback is difficult to elicit, because people fear the retaliation it could bring. The honesty of feedback is questionable, because, just as in the real world, we sometimes give compliments in order to received them.

The success of We Media thus far has been built on the evolution of reputations systems, trust metrics and the politics of social software. As the technology improves, facilitating better social connections, the future role of the mainstream media in this new media ecosystem comes into question.

Implications for Media and Journalism

The Internet has grown in a way distinctly different from any medium before it. As a result, it's difficult to predict how the Net will change mainstream media and to what magnitude. To say that media will undergo a "paradigm shift" might be an understatement. Consider that today 1 billion computers are connected to the Internet, most dialing in through telephone lines. By the end of 2010, Intel predicts that more than 1.5 billion computers will be connected via high-speed broadband and another 2.5 billion phones will have more processing power than today's PCs.

Yet, only one-tenth of the world's population, or 600 million people, can access the Internet today. What will happen when many of the rest join in seeking others with whom to collaborate and share information?

That's a revolution already underway, but it's one that's easy to miss. It's quiet. Revolutions on the Net happen at the edges, not at the center.

Economist J. Bradford Long explains: "As the action spreads from producers (the few) to users (the many), it becomes much, much harder to get an overview of the revolutionary things occurring. We have anecdotes of brilliant new uses and applications, but do they add up to an enduring boom or just a few isolated pops that make good copy?" And that is the problem facing media companies, the entertainment industry and even governments. How do you put together the pieces of a puzzle without knowing what the final picture looks like? First, you find the edges. While we may not be able predict how the media landscape will shift, there are places we can begin looking for change and their likely impacts.

Democratization of Media

Freedom of the press is guaranteed only to those who own one. Now, millions do. Those who believe the democratization of media will have little effect on big media often point to the "zine" business. In the late '80s and early '90s, desktop publishing allowed many small, independent publications to spring up. To some degree, the magazine business became more democratized with the addition of more viewpoints. But those publications generally expanded the reach of magazines without toppling the more established titles. In the same way, some see little evidence that micromedia will displace established media today.

An important distinction to remember is that the economics of production and distribution in the magazine business, while less costly than before, were still substantial - keeping the number of new competitors to a handful. Moreover, competing with magazines that had larger circulation usually required considerable marketing budgets and years to build a large subscriber base. On the Web, the barriers to entry are next to nothing. The costs associated with distributing content online are so low that anyone can join and experiment with the democratization of media.

And that experiment is quickly moving into the mainstream. Recently America Online announced it would get into the weblog game, putting simple and powerful publishing tools into the hands of more than 30 million members. Millions will own a press, making everyone a potential media outlet. With the ability to publish words and pictures even via their cell phone, citizens have the potential to observe and report more immediately than traditional media outlets do.

Challenges to the media

A democratized media challenges the notion of the institutional press as the exclusive, privileged, trusted, informed intermediary of the news. According to a recent Sports Illustrated story, "there is little doubt that fan websites are breaking - and making - news and dramatically reshaping the relationship between college coaches and the public. "Mainstream news media, SI included, monitor website message boards to take the public's pulse and, in some cases, look for news tips."

Are respected news operations such as SI likely to be eliminated as one of the primary intermediaries of sports news any time soon? That's unlikely, but Web communities and even search engines are becoming valued outlets of news, which guide and direct their readers to information of interest. The role these sites play - as filters, simplifiers and clarifiers of news - is adding a new intermediary layer. They might not be the ultimate authority, but the new intermediaries - forums, weblogs, search engines, hoax-debunking sites - are helping audiences sort through the abundance of information available today.

Many newspapers and TV stations have had years to establish the trust of their audiences. Yet participatory news sites, with their transparent and more intimate nature, are attracting legions of fans who contribute and collaborate with one another. In addition, recent surveys suggest people are beginning to place more trust in online sources and are seeking increasingly diverse news sources and perspectives.

What are the implications of a distributed, collective pool of knowledge on credibility? Arguably, the stakes go up. Online communities require transparency of sources and reporting methods. Experts emerge through the recognition of their online peers rather than by anointment by the mass media. For example, Glenn Fleishman, a freelance journalist in Seattle, has become one of the world's leading experts on wireless technology. He uses his weblog to both report on the latest developments in wi-fi and to interact with readers who might point him to a new wrinkle in the fast-moving field.

In a digital medium, reputations form through a synthesis of consistency, accuracy and frequent comparison by the reader. Individuals, institutions, the government and even reporters use the Web to maintain a record of their encounters with other media. The Department of Defense routinely posts transcripts of interviews with the Secretary of Defense and other high-ranking officials.

The motivation for self-publishing interviews appear to be twofold: To ensure that their words aren't misconstrued or misreported by the news media and to publish a complete public record of what the person being interviewed is saying. Even well-intentioned journalists may misinterpret an interviewee's meaning. Annotating provides the interviewee the opportunity to give his or her comments the kind of nuance, heft, context and thoughtfulness that might be left on the cutting-room floor in a news outlet's notoriously shrunken news hole.

One of the better examples of user-generated content actively challenging the media's credibility is product reviews. While mainstream readers might not actively seek news reports or political opinions from amateurs, many are willing to consult reviews contributed by strangers before they make a purchase. Commerce sites like Amazon or product review sites such as Epinions.com or Edmunds.com put a great deal of emphasis on user-generated reviews and discussions. Many manufacturing companies like Subaru have taken notice and actively monitor discussion boards to understand what online communities think about their products.

News organizations have spent much time and effort trying to position their journalists as more than impartial observers. They have in many ways tried to present them as experts in a field or interpreters of events. This approach in a print or broadcast model makes perfect sense. Online, the world of opinion and expert commentary is not restricted to the privileged. But forward-looking media companies don't view that development as a threat.

News organizations still have the resources to become known as the definitive authority on various subjects. They will have to make way, however, for readers who want pick up the tools of journalism to contribute to a more informed citizenry and a more robust democracy. For example, the news media and consumer non-profits no longer have a monopoly on serving as a watchdog on government and private industry. Individuals and citizen groups are stepping in to fill the void they believe has been created by lapses in coverage by big media.

Citizens are also taking up a media watchdog role when it comes to chronicling perceived evidence of the news media's political bias, censorship or reporting inaccuracies. Controversies surrounding the invasion of Iraq have fueled the launch of many sites. Mainstream media has been criticized for under-reporting both coalition force and Iraqi civilian casualties. In response, two sites - Iraq Coalition Casualty Count and Iraq Body Count - have attempted to establish independent databases that tabulate deaths by reviewing military and news reports. Each provides greater detail and accuracy than currently found in mainstream news reports. The sites also provide a transparency of sources and methodology rarely found in other media.

The Memory Hole, run by Russ Kick, is an example of a watchdog site that attempts to preserve and share information that has been removed from other sites on the Web or is difficult to find. FAIR.org scrutinizes media practices that "marginalize the public interest." Established in 1986, the organization highlights neglected news stories, opposes efforts at censorship and defends First Amendment precepts. In a similar vein, the Tyndall Report monitors the three major U.S. television networks' nightly newscasts and the time devoted to each story.

In England, where the BBC is funded by public tax monies, groups like bbcwatch.com have sprung up to make sure the broadcast organization stays true to its charter, which pledges journalism that is impartial and comprehensive. In the wake of corporate scandals and greater influence-peddling in Washington, grassroots organizations are also turning a watchful eye toward corporate responsibility. CommercialAlert.org, a 4-year-old consumer organization in Portland, Ore., tries "to keep the commercial culture within its proper sphere, and to prevent it from exploiting children and subverting the higher values of family, community, environmental integrity and democracy."

Three incidents in the spring of 2003 point to the disruptive effects that the Internet has begun to sow in newsrooms - a disruption that threatens the status quo of news organization culture and policy.

— In April 2003, The Hartford Courant required a travel editor and former columnist, Denis Horgan, to stop posting commentary to his weblog.

— A month earlier, CNN reporter Kevin Sites was told to discontinue posting to his blog, which featured first-hand accounts of the war in Iraq. According to a CNN spokesperson, "CNN.com prefers to take a more structured approach to presenting the news.... We do not blog."

— Similarly, Time magazine editors instructed reporter Joshua Kucera to stop posting reports from Kurdistan to his weblog.

The resistance in media organizations to these newer forms of expression is not surprising. But such incidents, which are likely to multiply, raise questions about the nature of the relationship between journalists and their employers. Is a journalist, by virtue of his or her newsroom employment and access to newsmakers, not permitted to express a personal opinion outside of the office? Do media companies own an employee's free time? Do such prohibitions apply only to working journalists or to newsroom executives as well?

A chief concern on the part of news organizations is one of liability. Allowing reporters to write when off the clock might expose a company to a lawsuit. In addition, news outlets may perceive a reporter's weblog as competition, since it potentially draws eyeballs away from a media company's advertisers. Yet, as media companies gear more of their operations to an online audience that expects a more interactive dynamic, things will have to change. The collaborative and fast-paced nature of online news will require new policies, technologies, organizational structures and workflows.

The assembly-line nature of broadcast and print media is not well-suited to developing content for smaller, more targeted audiences. Content will likely be published in a more continuous manner by teams or communities acting as an extention of the enterprise. Eventually, licensing and copyright policies will need to be reexamined to come into harmony with a collaborative audience model. Moreover, measuring and managing the success of such collaborative ventures might be a challenge and force some rethinking about how such projects are gauged within the larger organization.

Some news sites are experimenting on a small scale by co-opting successful participatory media models. MSNBC.com's Weblog Central section hosts a variety of analysts and columnists such as Instapundit.com's Glenn Reynolds and Eric Alterman of The Nation. Some of the more ambitious efforts have come from the United Kingdom. Whereas many larger news sites keep links to other sites to a minimum, Britain's The Guardian maintains many weblogs that guide readers to the best of the Web, including other news sites.

The BBC has announced plans to make its entire archives available for non-commercial use. Called the BBC Creative Archive, it will offer more than 80 years of radio and broadcast programs free to anyone. "In particular, it will be about how public money can be combined with new digital technologies to transform everyone's lives." When some media outlets start making participatory media work effectively, media companies that dig in their heels and resist such changes may be seen as not only old-fashioned but out of touch.

Assuming that issues related to newsroom culture can be overcome, there are more hurdles facing the media.

Along with a rethinking of journalism's role in the online medium, new skills and attitudes will be required. Staffs will need to be motivated to collaborate with colleagues, strangers, sources and readers. After years of working their way up the professional ladder, some reporters will undoubtedly need to discover a newfound respect for their readers. Arrogance and aloofness are deadly qualities in a collaborative environment.

To be successful, reporters will need to be more than skilled writers. They will have to hone their skills in growing communities around specific topics of interest. "That's one of the great challenges to us as news gatherers and journalists," said Joan Connell, executive producer for opinion and community at MSNBC.com. "How do we discover information and share it in creative ways with people? Give them the information they need to make the choices in their lives as citizens."

MSNBC.com believes that the editing process brings a higher degree of journalistic integrity to the news equation, and that's one factor that sets news organizations apart from personal weblogs. "One of the values that we place on our own weblogs is that we edit our webloggers. Out there in the blogosphere, often it goes from the mind of the blogger to the mind of the reader, and there's no backup....I would submit that that editing function really is the factor that makes it journalism."

Universities will also need to shape their journalism curricula to help students prepare for working in this new media ecosystem and the fast-changing tools needed. A larger unknown for investigative reporters will be the impact of the Internet on sources. Now that we live on the cusp of a world in which everyone has the potential to be a reporter and a source, will that affect the behavior of sources when they are approached by mainstream journalists?

Advertising and Marketing

Clay Shirky believes that mass media are dead. In his essay "RIP the Consumer 1900-1999," he suggests that mass media depend on two important characteristics of the audience: size and silence. According to recent Nielsen ratings reports, the TV audience continues to become more fragmented, with new channels continuing to proliferate. (Nightly network news viewership dropped in half from 1993 to 2002.) Today, an unqualified ratings champion is a fraction of what it was several years ago. Audiences, while still fairly large, are diminishing in size.

To Shirky, silence means that the audience remains passive. The Internet has helped to fracture mass media by empowering the audience to take a more active role when interacting with media. "The Internet heralds the disappearance of the consumer altogether," Shirky writes, "because the Internet destroys the noisy advertiser/silent consumer relationship that the mass media relies upon. The rise of the Internet undermines the existence of the consumer because it undermines the role of mass media. In the age of the Internet, no one is a passive consumer anymore because everyone is a media outlet."

There are a number of challenges facing media companies in the long run, if Shirky's argument is valid. First, traditional media may need to rethink how to measure economic success. One option is to explore avenues for targeted, personalized advertising aimed at individuals or small identifiable groups. Another is to consider the possibility of moving away from an advertising-supported business model and toward subscriptions and other pay-for-content models. Real-time data about readership and viewership might lead to new pricing rules where fixed pricing is replaced by real-time market adjustments.

In addition, media companies will likely have to devise new ways to present audiences to advertisers. Typically, standard demographics are the measure of an audience. It may be that more creative and descriptive measures of audiences, based around psychographic characteristics, will be devised. Such changes cannot happen without expecting a change in the relationship between businesses and their customers. While many news sites have experimented with personalization as a means to identify more targeted advertising opportunities, they have only fleetingly experimented with new ways to allow consumers to interact with advertisers.

Audiences and Stakeholders

Increasingly, audiences are becoming stakeholders in the news process. Rather than passively accepting news coverage decided upon by a handful of editors, they fire off emails, post criticism of perceived editorial shortcomings on weblogs and in forums, and support or fund an independent editorial enterprise. In June 2000 the NOW Legal Defense and Education Fund launched Women's eNews, a news service run by a small staff of professional journalists who work with a national network of free-lance writers. Devoted to coverage of women's issues, the site became a fully independent operation in early 2002. In July 2003 it won four journalism awards from the National Federation of Press Women and continues to probe issues often overlooked by the mainstream media.

Occasionally, readers will dig into their own pockets to finance a journalism effort they find worthwhile. Freelance journalist Christopher Allbritton received $14,334 from 320 people who funded his trip to Iraq to report his first-hand observations of the war zone. He filed daily dispatches on his Web site, Back-to-Iraq.com, about the fall of Tikrit and reported on the region's ethnic tensions. A freelance journalist from Maine, David Appel, asked readers of his weblog to pony up to let him pursue an investigative story. After receiving more than $200, Appel investigated a sugar lobbying group's attempt to get Congress to kill funding for the World Health Organization, whose policies had offended corporate sugar interests.

While war reporting and investigative reporting remain the province of trained journalists, more often citizens are taking up the tools of journalism to write about favorite topics. Columnist J.D. Lasica calls these do-it-yourself entries "random acts of journalism," as when Jessica Rios, a 22-year-old woman in Los Angeles, attended a Coldplay concert and wrote a review of their performance on her weblog. The author Howard Rheingold is representative of a new kind of reader who spends more time with favorite weblogs and collaborative media than with traditional media. "The things I'm interested in, from pop culture to wireless policy to copyright, you have to go to the fanatics," he said. And those fanatics are more easily found in niche online media.

Potential Benefits of We Media

Participatory journalism is not going to disappear any time soon. Communication, collaboration and sharing personal passions have been at the heart of the Internet since its inception more than 30 years ago. David Weinberger, author of Small Pieces Loosely Joined, says that this is because the Web is not just a giant marketplace or an information resource. Rather, "it's a social commons on which the interests of a mass of individuals are splayed in universally accessible detail and trumpeted in an effectively infinite array of personal voices."

According to Scott Rosenberg, managing editor of Salon.com, what Weinberger reminds us is that "every Web site, every Internet posting matters to the person who created it - and maybe to that person's circle of site visitors, whether they number 10 million or just 10." "Individually, these contributions may be crude, untrustworthy, unnoteworthy. Collectively, they represent the largest and most widely accessible pool of information and entertainment in human history. And it's still growing."

If media companies are going to collaborate with their audiences online, they must begin to consider a news and information Web site as a platform that supports social interaction around the stories they create. These interactions are as important as the narrative, perhaps more so, because they are created and owned by the audience. In a networked world, media whose primary value lies in its ability to connect people will win.

This section explores the potential benefits to media companies and businesses that adopt participatory journalism in meaningful ways. Possible examples include enabling editors and reporters to publish a weblog about the subjects they cover; hosting, moderating and participating in discussion forums or groups about news; encouraging audience contribution of editorial content for distribution on a Web site or in a traditional media product; enabling your readers to purchase online advertising through affordable text ads. The possibilities are limitless, as long as it includes an effort to engage the audience in an authentic conversation and collaboration. An involved, empowered audience could well bring a number of potential benefits to media companies.

According to a USA Today/CNN/Gallup Poll in June 2003, only 36 percent of those polled believe the news media generally "get the facts straight." News media have their work cut out in restoring their reputations and their readers' sense of trust. Participatory journalism provides media companies with the potential to develop a more loyal and trustworthy relationship with their audiences. This can happen, for example, with a reporter who writes a weblog, asking the audience to fuel her efforts by providing tips, feedback and first-hand accounts that confirm a story's premise or that take it in a different direction.

We Media can also provide the audience a deeper level of understanding about the reporting process by illustrating, for example, how a reporter must balance competing interests. This communication can lead to a lasting trust. Time magazine media critic James Poniewozik explains how this is possible, when he describes the perception gap between the audience and the media about trust. "Journalists think trust equals accuracy. But it's about much more: passion, genuineness, integrity." Honest conversation and passionate collaboration could instill respect and trust into the relationship between both parties. Involving an audience, either small or large, in the creation of content also gives them a sense of ownership - an affinity with the media brand that they believe they are not getting today - as well as a more intimate relationship with the storytellers.

An audience that participates in the journalistic process is more demanding than passive consumers of news. But they may also feel empowered to make a difference. As a result, they feel as though they have a shared stake in the end result. According to Bill Kovach and Tom Rosenstiel, authors of the book The Elements of Journalism, citizens must take an active, collaborative role in the journalistic process if we are to realize an effective journalism that appropriately informs a democracy.

"Journalists must invite their audience into the process by which they produce the news," Kovach and Rosenstiel write in their book. "They should take pains to make themselves and their work as transparent as they insist on making the people and institutions of power they cover. This sort of approach is, in effect, the beginning of a new kind of connection between the journalist and the citizen. It is one in which individuals in the audience are given a chance to judge the principles by which the journalists do their work."

"The first step in that direction has to be developing a means of letting those who make up that market finally see how the sausage is make - how we do our work and what informs our decisions." Many journalists who are already weblogging are doing just that - exposing the raw material of their stories-in-progress, posting complete text of interviews after the story is published, and inviting comments, fact checking and feedback that contribute to follow-up stories.

Online interactive experiences are more memorable than relatively static experiences such as newspapers, according to Web usability expert Jakob Nielsen. "Moving around is what the Web is all about," Nielsen explains. "When analyzing the 'look-and-feel' of a website, the feel completely dominates the user experience. After all, doing is more memorable and makes a stronger emotional impact than seeing."

Collaborating and having a conversation with audience members is sure to provide an even more meaningful and memorable experience than passive consumption of news. Likewise, enabling your audience to talk about and extend news stories also increases retention and understanding. When we read a story that grabs us, we want to tell others, who will also likely tell others. Good stories are inherently infectious. Sharing and discussing them is a natural extension of the experience.

"As users have greater effect upon the experience, they become more absorbed (immersed) in the experience," according to the authors of a research study, "Interactive Features of Online Newspapers." "What users do with content is more important than how content may affect users. Users are actively chasing discovery, rather than passively being informed." Ultimately, the authors argue, "journalists today must choose. As gatekeepers they can transfer lots of information, or they can make users a smarter, more active and questioning audience for news events and issues."

News Consumers in New Generation

Increasing interactivity and enabling audience participation have an additional benefit - attracting a younger audience, the next generation of news consumers. Kids today expect to interact with their media. From playing interactive online games, to using instant messenger (IM) services to communicate with friends, to interacting with their television (by having control over when programs are watched, and skipping commercials with devices like TiVo and ReplayTV), today's kids expect their media to offer a two-way street of communication.

A safe assumption is that when today's children and teenagers reach adulthood, they'll not be tolerant of media that's one-way, that's not interactive. They expect to be able to manipulate media content, and to share it with others. The one-way conversation of a printed newspaper won't do

- thus print's prospects for the young digital generation are not promising. Newspaper Web sites and other newspaper digital media formats likewise cannot afford to perpetuate the one-way model. They've got to become more interactive.

An interesting question, yet to be addressed by research in this field, is: Does participatory journalism - the process of collaboration and conversation between media and the audience - ultimately help create better stories and better storytellers?

"I've found that my readers definitely know more than I do, and, to my benefit, they share their knowledge," says San Jose Mercury News technology columnist Dan Gillmor, who has been writing a weblog since 1999. Based on Gillmor's experience and that of others in the field, reporters who write weblogs and collaborate with their audiences in various ways ultimately write more compelling and accurate stories. One reason is that listening to and collaborating with your audience helps to develop a broader base of sources who are experts in wide-ranging subject matter.

The Internet as it wires millions of individuals as potential information experts into a global communications infrastructure provides an ideal platform for improving journalism by incorporating the expertise of people 'outside of the Rolodex.' Voice and personality are also key hallmarks of participatory media. Several observers have argued that the informal style found in many participatory forms free the writer from the "official voice" of the media company, and that makes for better storytelling. The official voice of journalism is usually formal, often drained of color and attitude, and written as an objective and balanced account.

In contrast, weblogs and discussion groups thrive on their vivid writing, controversial points of view and personality-rich nature - traits that many readers find compelling. Columnist J.D. Lasica goes so far as to argue that newspaper webloggers should not be subject to the newsroom's routine editing filter. On his weblog he called for a form of Editing Lite: "Perhaps the chief appeal and attraction of weblogs are their free-form, unfiltered nature. You get to hear people in their natural dialect, writing from their gut with a voice and tone that too often can be filtered into a homogenous blandness after passing through the typical newsroom's editing machine. A lightly edited, hands-off weblog would show journalists as human beings with opinions, emotions and personal lives."

Audience participation serves another salutary function. The mainstream media tend to dispose of stories in a fast-paced news cycle. Even important news events often fall off the media's radar screen after 48 hours. The blogosphere and discussion forums keep stories alive by recirculating them and regurgitating them with new angles or insights. Weblogs have been credited with keeping in the public spotlight Sen. Trent Lott's statement expressing fondness for the Dixiecrat era of one-time segregationist Strom Thurmond, a controversy that led to Lott stepping down as Senate majority leader.

Scalable Virtual Staff

An involved audience can play the role of a scalable virtual staff - a massive pool of grassroots writers, commentators, photographers and videographers. Collaborating with them enables media to be and go where they normally cannot, due to geography or cost. For example, in the weeks leading up to the Iraq war, BBC News asked its worldwide audience to send in digital images from anti-war protests held around the globe, then published a slide show of the best images on its Web site.

Traditionally, media companies have viewed the concept of online community no differently than a section of a newspaper or a segment of a newscast. It is something that has been segregated from the news - a closed-off annex where readers can talk and discuss, as long as the media companies don't have to be too involved. Such an architected virtual space is not a true online community. Real communities have leaders, moderators and involved participants who care about their space.

Network Identity

In the past 10 years there have been numerous scientific discoveries about how networks form and behave. This has led us to understand that networks are driven by hubs and nodes. News media have traditionally viewed themselves as central nodes in the information network, with the power to control the ebb and flow of news. On the Web, that is no longer possible. News sites that sit behind registration firewalls, or whose content is quickly moved into paid archives, display the characteristics of a cul-de-sac rather than a connected node on a network. Adopting various forms of participatory journalism will increase the importance of your company's hub in the network economy. By increasing the number of connections - though weblogs, forums, XML syndication and collaborative publishing engines - the strength of a media company's node is enhanced.

How Media Might Respond

Media organizations will need to rethink some of their basic ideas about journalism, organization and the role of audience if they hope to remain indispensable resources to their readers and viewers. There are three types of connections that media should consider:

1. *Continuous connections*: Magazines and newspapers need Internet counterparts that are providing continuous updates to their audience. This doesn't mean, a web site filled with shovelware content. It needs to be a 24x7x365, living, breathing, responsive extension of your brand. Increase the frequency of connections with daily email newsletters, weblogs, RSS feeds and forums.

2. *Network connections, online and off*: Use your content (print and online) as a platform to guide and direct readers to additional news, information and experiences on the Web and in other media. Ultimately, this will make your content more valuable because it's connected to similar information. As well, your customers' media diet is becoming more varied and vast. Don't leave your product in a cul-de-sac.

3. *Intercast connections*: A successful news Web site is a platform that supports social interaction around the story. Print media must begin to engage and grow online community in order to build affinity and loyalty to their brand experience. Community members have a stake in your brand when they engage the journalistic process - by providing valuable commentary, displaying their mastery of a subject, offering grassroots reporting and acting as filters for their fellow readers.

News organizations have policies, practices and traditions that discourage connections. Despite this, the audience is still managing to become part of the news equation by creating links and commentary that center on news events. The emergent behavior of participatory journalism suggests that audiences want to create intimate connections with news organizations, reporters and the stories they produce. The challenge in newsrooms will be to persuade writers, editors and advertisers to stop thinking in terms of a broadcast model (one-to-many) and to start "thinking network" (one-to-one).

According to Albert-László Barabási, author of Linked: The New Science of Networks, media organizations are tree networks. "The CEO sits at the root and the bifurcating branches represent the increasingly specialized and nonoverlapping tasks of lower-level manager and workers," Barabási writes. "Responsibility decays as you move down the branches, ending with drone executors of orders conceived at the roots. This is the standard model of corporations, one that has been ingrained in their DNA for more than 100 years.

"These days, however, the value is in ideas and information," Barabási writes. "As companies face an information explosion and an unprecedented need for flexibility in a rapidly changing marketplace, the corporate model is in the midst of a complete makeover. "The most visible element of this remaking is a shift from a tree to a web or network organization, flat and with lots of cross-links between the nodes."

The internal remaking of media companies, transforming them from tree organizations into web networks, is only one consequence of a network economy, Barabási says. "Another is the realization that companies never work alone. They collaborate with other institutions, adapting business practices proved successful in other organizations." In the case of participatory journalism, this means that media companies will increasingly collaborate with their audience, either directly in a one-on-one fashion, or indirectly using audience-created communities such as Slashdot.org leads for story generation.

But none of this will happen unless the media organization and its business culture are transformed. Such a radical change will not occur overnight. This is uncharted territory for most and large-scale change in corporations is fraught with pitfalls. With media companies still generating respectable returns on investment, the smart money will be on those organizations that can integrate successful experiments supported by better staff training, equipment and practices that encourage reporters and editors to interact with their audience.

Media companies must consider that the role of reporters and editors are in flux. Audience wants a closer relationship with the storytellers. Reporters and editors must find the proper balance between encouraging audience participation and producing something ready for publication or broadcast - and finding that balance may prove difficult. Reporters and editors will need to be empowered to grow communities of interest online. As the value of their communities grows so will it enhance the value of the media organization.

However, we are increasingly seeing media companies force their employees to make the choice between their jobs and their weblogs, rather than trying to determine how blogging can serve the interests of both parties. Such controlling behavior on the part of media companies sends a negative message to their audiences. Readers begin to wonder, "If journalists cannot be heard, then what is the media company hiding?" Weblogs are an excellent way for staff members and readers to bridge the communication gap.

A key component of what makes a good journalist, according to Bill Kovach and Tom Rosenstiel, is an obligation to personal conscience. "Every journalist - from the newsroom to the boardroom - must have a personal sense of ethics and responsibility - a moral compass," they say in their book The Elements of Journalism. "What's more, they have a responsibility to voice their personal conscience out loud and allow others around them to do so as well. "The top-down structure of oligarchies usually makes it more difficult for individuals to be heard on abstract matters, such as ethics or questions of conscience. As long as we have one newspaper and only three or four TV stations doing news in most cities, we cannot rely solely on the marketplace to protect journalism ethics."

But providing journalists with some measure of autonomy goes beyond questions of ethics and conscience. Such a move can lead to more compelling stories, fostering a closer relationship between audience and storyteller, outside of the classic construct of a newspaper or TV station. Ultimately, the audience develops an allegiance to those who are authentic and open in their pursuit of journalism. News organizations and audiences will have to become more comfortable with a duality they have wrestled with for years - journalist as objective observer and as an informed conscience.

Critical to any participatory model is the understanding that the audience needs to play a meaningful role in the news process. Ohmynews.com relies upon thousands of citizen journalists to produce the majority of the site's daily content. While that model might appear extreme to many traditional news organizations, it illustrates that there are thousands of people eager to contribute to the news equation. Publications such as the Santa Fe New Mexican, Dallas Morning News and BBC

News have taken a step in that direction by soliciting reader photographs, news accounts and other user-generated content.

News organizations also need to consider how to empower the audience as a valued intermediary of the news. When deciding on what news to read, the audience often trusts other audience members for recommendations before they trust an editor. Thus, the popularity of "most-read and most-emailed stories" pages on news sites. Likewise, this is one of the reasons why weblogs are useful. Weblogs act as a filter on the news, helping its audience cut through the fat of the news and get to what's important to them. News organizations face a challenge in deciding the extent to which they want to leverage audience participation and incorporate it into their news products.

According to a Harvard Business Review article on turning your customers into innovators, organizations need to provide some type of free toolkit to effectively collaborate with their customers. Here's what a customer collaboration toolkit for news media might contain:

Open-source style guide: One of the hidden parts of journalism is style. If media are going to enable its audience to produce news and information, then it behooves media to educate its audience on the best ways to produce it. Why not make your style guide open source? Being accurate, reliable and consistent has value, and something like an open-source style guide is critical to infecting social networks with the power to adopt journalism's best practices. The BBC offers its style guide online along with journalism courses. Many universities also post their style guides online.

Provide a journalism learning program: For those audience members who really want to become full-fledged journalists, a learning program is the next step. Such a program would encompass writing, editing, audio, video and still photography. Participants should do more than take notes; they should report on an event and then engage in a group discussion that examines best practices. Such a course also must include an ethics guide. Certification, or graduation, could be a requirement for a participant to become a "trusted" contributor. Media might consider adopting a program similar to MIT's OpenCourseWare, which includes lecture notes, video lectures, simulations and lab courses.

Encourage low-cost content management solutions: Large newspaper sites use expensive and complicated content management systems, but that doesn't mean their audience should, too. Encourage audience members to create their own content. This, in turn, will make a more fertile ground for your content. If you cannot provide the publishing tools for them, guide them to open-source tools or other reasonable platforms. Consider offering Web services, as Amazon, eBay and Google do, to provide audiences with a way to create new products that enhance your news and information. Some blogging tools, such as MovableType, have features that provide notifications when someone has commented on a story. Integrating such functionality in news sites can greatly increase the interest and goodwill of communities.

The last and perhaps most important step for a media company to take is to relinquish control. News media are geared to own a story. They shape it, package it and sell it. But that mindset might make organization blind to the larger opportunity. Today, news media organizations are actually story instigators. They track down important stories and relay them to the world. Once they are released, stories transform and can take a life of their own beyond the control of the news organization.

The Internet community (and other media) appropriates the stories, retells them, comments on them, adds additional information or overlooked angles, and reworks them as part of a broad-based web of ideas and information. That's not only a good thing, it's essential. If it's not happening, it means your reporting has little value to your audience. If journalism is indeed about informing the community and lifting up our fellow citizens, we need to evolve. We need to tell better stories and, while doing so, we need to engage the world.

8

NGOs and Media Advocacy

Non-profit Organisations Needs Publicity

One of the primary ways a non-profit organization tells its story to its key audiences is through the press. You may not have a major television station in your area, but chances are you have a local newspaper, a local radio station, and perhaps a local-access cable television station. Before long, you also will be using the Internet, whether you post your news on someone else's World Wide Web site or develop your own.

Media relations is only one part of a public relations plan, but it can be your most valuable and efficient tool. Once you know how to get your message not only accepted, but valued, as important news by your local media, you've made a big step toward the success of your program. Publicity is not only low cost but has high return. Placing a news story about your event or your organization gives your message credibility and recognition, whether broadcast or printed.

Good editors and news directors, however, appreciate timely, well-written and well-organized news releases and will use them appropriately. They also like story tips that they can follow up on their own time. But don't ask for blatant advertising to be treated as news. News professionals are very adept at recognizing real news and culling out thinly disguised ads. They know their audiences, and they know their continuation as a business depends upon advertising sales.

Basic Guidelines

The first skill to develop is to recognize the difference between news and advertising. Do that by reading, listening and watching the local media to see how they treat news so that you can conform to their choices and styles. News is something unusual or important and/or affects a large number of people in a significant way. It must be timely. For example: Don't announce your relocation after you are settled in. Feature stories also should be timely. If you keep on top of what's in the news you might be able to tie today's headlines to something in your collections. If your part of the state is bracing for a flood, what do you have in your collections that tell the stories of past floods?

When the Legislature wrangles with school funding issues, can you find the records of a country school that operated on a small salary for a teacher, some slates and a pile of firewood? When June dairy days roll around, can you write a short piece on your collection of cream separators, or cowbells? Or offer to let the local paper photograph these pieces of history?

Second, learn to write good news releases. Put the news in the first paragraph; don't hide it under a paragraph about your organization (that goes last). Be brief, be clear, and be accurate. Neatness counts. Proofread three times, not just for typographical errors, but for content. Make sure your release has the "who, what, when, where, why and how" within the text. Every name must be spelled correctly. Using a quote from a credible source is great, but make sure it is lively.

Double space your copy. Indicate the end with a mark or the symbols. If your release goes over one page in length use "more" at the bottom to indicate to typesetters that they should look for the rest of the release. But don't write more than two pages. Newspaper space is valuable. Broadcasters will cut your news release to fit a very small time frame. You might want to write shorter releases for local radio stations. If they take Public Service Announcements, or PSAs, the rule of thumb is that a minute is filled with 150 words maximum, and no PSA should be more than a minute. Be sure to put the name of the person editors can call for more information at the top.

Third, learn media deadlines so your releases reach the right place at the right time. No one appreciates working at the last minute, and sometimes there just isn't room for late news.

Fourth, get to know your local press so that when you have a good story idea, they will listen and follow through.

Media Relations Sound

If media relations sounds like a big job, it is. But it can be organized into a job that can be handled by a volunteer. The key is timely information flow within the organization. Your publicity chairperson must have information early so he or she isn't rushed into providing the press with a hastily written release or one that is nearly too late to print. Part of the planning for any event, new acquisition or any major project should include a plan for publicity.

Designate someone to provide accurate information to the publicity chairperson by a specific deadline-at least one month prior to when you plan to hold your event or make an announcement. This information could be on a form designed to capture the essential "who, what, when, where, why and how" information from the project manager. It should also have a phone number that will be published in the release as a number the public can call for more information. Information about outside funding sources and sponsors also is appropriate. Although your local editor might rewrite your release, if the information is printed, your release has done its job.

Organizations that receive public funding have a duty to let the public know what they are doing and how to access their programs. That makes media relations one of the most important roles of your organization. Take the time to do it right and it will return good will, attendance at events, recognition for your organization and a chance to promote the appreciation of history through the media.

The natural reaction is to start trying to get more publicity. And part of the purpose of this booklet is to help you do just that. But first things first: you need to answer some important questions before you begin planning a publicity campaign.

Goals of the Organization

Developing a clear statement of the organiztion's mission is the essential first step. When this is accomplished, a set of short-term goals will enable you to direct the organization's energy toward achieving your mission successfully. Development of goals (which may require you to convince the membership that it can't go forward without establishing a direction) leads ot questions related to publicity:

— Why do we need publicity?

— What is your group trying to accomplish that would benefit from others' awareness?

— Who—specifically—do we need to talk to in order to succeed?

— Who is the audience?

— What do we want to say to them?

— What is the message?

— What are the best vehicles for our message?

— How can I get the word out in the most direct, efficient way?

Unless you can come up with concrete answers to these questions, your hard work may not yield tangible benefits... just clippings. Your organization's logo or other identification can be used very dramatically and in fun ways to keep your name before the public.

Most non-profit groups have at least two target audiences — the people who use their services and those whose contributions of volunteer labor, cash or in-kind contributions enable the program to survive. The most effective communications with each of these groups may be very different, indeed. making sure potential users of your service know how to gain access to it is one important message. Another is that your effective use of cash contributions has produced a tangible benefit for the community and for the donor. Still another might be that your group provides meaningful opportunities for volunteer involvement.

While media relations has its place in your public relations plan, it is just one element of a solid P.R. program. It's always satisfying to see one's name in the paper. But your overall objective should be to ensure a steady flow of information to your constituents through a variety of channels. That means integrating your media activities with other public relations/communications tools to keep your visibility high among consumers, volunteers, current and potential contributors, public officials, and other groups or agencies which might lend support.

Public Relations Planning

The most common pitfall in the practice of public relations is the vain hope that one newspaper story or one all-purpose brochure will create all the public awareness your group will ever need. communication is an on-going process, comprised 10% of the big and splashy and 90% of the slow, persistent and consistent broadcasting of a few key points. It's taking every opportunity to seek out potential consumers or supporters and tell them why your group's work is important to them and how they can be involved.

When developing your public relations plan, the more specific goals you have the more effective you'll be. "Get more publicity" isn't nearly specific enough. If your organization needs to increase ticket sales by 20 percent, for example, your public relations plan needs to focus on media and other communications channels most likely to reach potential ticket buyers. You need to define who those ticket buyers are and what message, carried in what format, has the greatest likelihood of persuading them to buy tickets.

Your volunteers and employees at work in a dramatic environment such as this is attention-getting! Combined with a press release or just a photo caption which explains the who, what, where and when of the subject may be just what your local newspaper is looking for. For example, if you offer a program aimed at adolescent boys (who all drive cars) and you want them to make fuller use of your program, you might want to create flyers or posters for distribution through auto parts stores and service stations.

Next, it's important to try to accomplish only one objective per promotional message. If you want to increase program use, don't also try to raise funds for your program and recruit volunteers in the same promotional piece. Create separate promotional activities for each distinct target audience and message.

Finally, be alert for opportunities to create working relationships with other non-profit or for-profit groups who can furnish consumers, volunteers or even contributors to your program - and vice versa. Your program for adolescent boys might be of great interest to the high school guidance counselor, Parents Without Partners, even juvenile officers. When you're defining "who" to talk to, be as inclusive as possible. Count as potential supporters all the professionals who regularly deal with your target consumers, the organizations which share an interest in them or serve them in some other way. Perhaps you can strengthen each other.

Among the most useful elements or tools for creating a solid public relations campaign are these:

Mailing Lists are worth their weight in gold if they are broken into constituent categories (that includes consumers, supporters and media) and if you keep them updated.

Newsletters you produce can cover the good news that's interesting to your constituents but not necessarily to the mass media. Your newsletter is the place to include consumer profiles, salute volunteers and contributors, outline upcoming activities and thank the repairman who fixed your office equipment at no charge. Thanking such supporters publicly encourages further support. And it's impressive to potential donors, who often not only want to see that other companies underwrite your activities but also that you generate grassroots support.

Brochures are greatly favored by any organization, and they have their uses. But funds should be allocated for a newsletter first because it's an on-going communication whereas a brochure appears only once. "Go for reach and frequency" is an advertising principle that underscores the importance of consistent, targeted communication. "Reach" refers to the number of members of your target audience that will be exposed to your message. "Frequency" refers to the number of times your message is repeated. Thus, the brochure targets a single message — one time. The newsletter allows you to change the message frequently and continuously.

Audio-Visual Presentations of five minutes or less (either in slide-show or videotape format) can prove useful in many settings: as part of community service fairs, on fundraising calls, at presentations to clubs and organizations. Always keep duplicates in case of loss or the need to be represented in two places at once.

Speakers Bureaus can bring a representative of your group before clubs, churches, service organizations and professional groups which might share an interest in the service you provide. Poll your members and professionals working in the field to determine their willingness to speak both to your group. Then contact groups whose support would be beneficial to your organization to see if a speaker might be scheduled. Follow up on the bookings, keep a list of equipment and power requirements, make sure your speaker is certain of the time, place and directions and ask for feedback after the talk.

Exhibits can be assembled from photographs, clippings, existing audio-visual presentations and memorabilia from your group and used at a variety of public gatherings.

Special Events, Open Houses and Tours, especially if demonstrations are incorporated, allow old friends and potential new ones to see your organization in action.

Billboards and Bus Cards can often be arranged free or at lower non-profit rates (you pay for artwork and printing). Contact the billboard company or transportation agency's public service director.

Flyers and Posters can be placed in homes, stores, community centers, libraries and spots with public bulletin boards. Cleverly designed, they can also serve as mailers to patrons, or, with the addition of a wooden stake they become yard signs.

Service-Learning Integration in a Public Relations Programme

Most professional programs, like public relations, focus on societal needs. Equally important is the skill attainment of students in such programs. Therefore, experiential learning, particularly service learning, appears to be an ideal pedagogy for professionally oriented programs. Students gain a deeper understanding of their power to influence and contribute to society, and they are better able to perfect their classroom-taught skills.

Service learning could also have a major impact on public relations education. Public relations graduates to have a broad-based liberal arts background; knowledge of concepts like strategic planning and issues management; and the ability to research, communicate effectively and think critically. But professionals want much more. They want public relations graduates who can write releases, develop media lists, construct questionnaires, create publications, and compose backgrounders with little or no instruction. They want graduates with well-developed portfolios and practical experience that will shorten the learning curve in their new positions.

Many public relations programs have opportunities for students to acquire practical experience. Most encourage internships and offer campaigns courses in which students develop work for a client. Nevertheless, many public relations students still enter the workforce with limited skills and practical know-how. Service learning, however, can strengthen public relations education from a critical perspective. This pedagogy can help students enrich their appreciation and understanding of the interests of stakeholders and the importance of social responsibility – key concepts in public relations education.

The service-learning movement can be an opportune time for public relations programs to seize the moment by embracing service learning, thereby giving their students more ways to develop their skills, apply course concepts in real-life situations, and enhance their understanding of social responsibility. In journalism and mass communication, few studies have focused on the nature of student-community partner relationships and their outcomes.

Over the years, definitions of public relations have changed to reflect the growing sophistication and maturation of the practice. Cutlip and Center defined public relations as "the planned effort to influence opinion through good character and responsible performance, based on mutually satisfactory two-way communication". Even the first-established public relations counselors understood the importance of good deeds and responsible performance. Considered the father of public relations, Ivy Lee saw the need for organizations to respond to public opinion and align themselves with the public interest.

Lee is credited with recognizing that good publicity is generated from good works and performance. Likewise, Edward Bernays called for "a movement toward public responsibility in private business". He believed that organizations need to recognize changes in their social setting and must respond to those changes in order to meet a common ground with stakeholders.

Social Responsibility in Public Relations

During the industrial revolution, business was concerned with profit-making and had few government controls. Social responsibility began to evolve as a concept in the 1960s in response to society's changing social values. Public policy debates of the 1960s and 1970s raised awareness of social issues. Legislative agencies were established. Corporations had new legal responsibilities, and public expectations for the social accountability of business heightened.

Social issues surfaced, such as equal employment opportunities, the environment, and product safety. Federal cutbacks in the 1980s forced business to expand and redefine its obligation to society. Business was pressured not only to support social causes but also to consider the social consequences of its activities.

Social responsibility is the development of processes to evaluate stakeholder and environmental demands and the implementation of programs to manage social issues. Corporate social responsibility deals with ethical codes, corporate philanthropy, community relations programs, and law-abiding actions. Corporations are responsible for effectively producing and distributing goods and services for consumer consumption and generating profits for stakeholders. However, society also feels that corporations should contribute to worthy social causes.

Corporations became viewed as both economic and social institutions. As social institutions, corporations have responsibilities to society. In fact, some scholars argue that all organizations – profit-making and nonprofit-making – have an obligation to society. Organizations exist at the pleasure of society, and society expects organizations to anticipate and resolve social problems. Since social responsibility is a key concept in public relations education, service learning is an ideal teaching strategy.

As future public relations practitioners in business and nonprofit organizations, students must realize their responsibility to society as they make decisions about the policies affecting their stakeholders (e.g., employees, residents of the local community, and government agencies). Confusion about the meaning of service learning abounds among public relations and other mass communication educators. Service learning is often mistaken for other forms of community-based, experiential-learning methods.

Community-based learning encompasses many different activities: working as a volunteer for a charitable institution; conducting field work or developing a thesis through independent study; taking an internship to gain on-the-job experience; enrolling in cooperative education to work in a paid, off-campus environment; participating in a short-term course-related activity; developing a community-based assignment for a course, such as conducting research or shadowing a professional for a day; and being a service-learning, which combines meaningful community service and in-class learning through a process of structured, regular reflections.

Service learning is a teaching method that blends community service and academic instruction through reflective, critical thinking. Student learning is promoted through community service experiences that meet the needs of a particular group, include structured activities for students to reflect on their experiences, and enhance students' academic studies. Service learning involves using course concepts and applying them in a real-life setting for the good of society.

Some scholars strongly assert that service learning requires a reflection component where students think critically about their experiences. Commonly used methods of reflection include journals, writing assignments and group discussions. The result of service learning is experience for students – honing their abilities and perfecting their skills – and an appreciation of good citizenship. The organization benefiting from the efforts of the service-learner receives much-needed skills and volunteer time. Thus, service-learning can be seen as a win-win situation for both the service-learning and the organization benefiting from a student's work.

Many researchers have documented the benefits of service learning. Simply put, service learning promotes social and moral responsibility, helps students become more involved in their communities, and impacts students' belief in the importance of social justice and the need for public policy change. For students, service learning helps then learn the course material, enables students to better identify issues in their community and act on them, and heightens their sense of citizenship. Plus, it introduces them to the complexity of the world.

Undergraduates develop a stronger sense of competence, are more likely to graduate, get better grades, be more favorably predisposed and connected to the educational institution, and feel as though they are living up to their potential. Bourland and Fall found that students saw service learning as lasting learning, an effective form of pedagogy. Students develop academically and cognitively by increasing their ability to write, read and calculate; subject matter knowledge; and critical-thinking skills and by becoming engaged learners.

Students also like service learning. They report that service learning increases their self-knowledge and spiritual growth, and it offers them opportunities to develop close personal relationships with fellow students. Students believe their learning is richer and more applicable to real-world contexts than traditional classroom experiences. Faculty who embrace service learning tend to value the meaning and purpose of their endeavors and enjoy positive feedback from students and colleagues; yet they struggle with varying student skill level, an increased time factor, and challenges in evaluating student work.

Service learning can renew an instructor's love of teaching. Most faculty reward systems fail to acknowledge the contributions of faculty engaged in service-learning pedagogy. Rather, other traditional forms of teaching and scholarship are given more consideration and weight in matters of retention, tenure and promotion.

Integration of Service Learning

Service learning was embraced by the campus community at California State University-Long Beach when the institution joined the Campus Compact, a coalition of college and university presidents committed to helping students develop the values of citizenship through participation in community service. Cal State-Long Beach is a large urban, comprehensive university located in Southern California. Public relations majors number around 130 and are required to fulfill the same curriculum prescribed by the Commission on Public Relations Education for a public relations program.

Experiential learning has long been included in the program through two required courses – "Internship" and "Public Relations Agency," which is a campaigns course. To receive credit for an internship, students must apply course concepts at the work site. Most of the work produced by students helps develop their skills. Therefore, specific job tasks must focus on writing, production and research, rather than clerical work. Site supervisors must be public relations professionals with five years of experience, be at the managerial level, and sign an agreement to mentor the student. In the agency course, students work in teams to develop a comprehensive public relations campaign for an actual client.

In both experiential-learning courses, students refine their skills and produce work that can be displayed in their portfolios. But, as most professors realize, the more experience and opportunities to apply course concepts in real-life settings, the more demonstration of higher-order learning processes and mastery. Therefore, the public relations program at Cal State-Long Beach looked seriously at the possibilities offered through service learning. Not only did service learning give students more opportunities to refine their skills, it provided a way to enrich their appreciation of the importance of social responsibility – a key public relations concept.

A natural place to integrate service learning into the public relations curriculum came easily in the skills courses – three required courses in the major after students completed their foundation courses. The skills courses are "Internal Communication for Public Relations," "External Communication for Public Relations" and "Publications for Public Relations." In these skills courses, students create public relations tools – a crisis communication plan, press kit, brochure and newsletter – for a nonprofit organization in need of such materials.

In the "Public Relations Agency" course, students work in teams to create a comprehensive public relations plan for a nonprofit organization and also pair with another community partner on an individual basis to develop a plan tailored to the unique needs of that organization. In each course, students approach a nonprofit of their choice. Once the organization is approved by the instructor, the contact at the nonprofit institution, usually the agency's director, and student sign a service-learning contract, outlining expectations for both parties.

Integrating service learning into the curriculum of public relations programs appears to be an ideal method to train students to become adept in the skills needed for the workplace and to shape their value system so they will perform their work in a socially responsible way. Since few service-learning studies have focused on outcomes for both student and community partner and little research exists on service learning in mass communication education, particularly public relations, research is needed to explore these issues in more depth.

Publics of Public Relations

There have been numerous definitions of public relations. Most small organizations do not have senior-level public relations professionals working on their team, so that leaves the job to someone with many other duties, such as a museum manager, or to a volunteer, who might be anywhere on the scale from entry-level to pro.

PR is both an art and a science—essentially it means being aware of your audiences (your "publics") and planning policies and actions that serve the interest of both the organization and the public.

Advertising is space purchased or time purchased to deliver a message prepared by the purchaser.

Publicity is information supplied to a news medium without cost. The decision to use it and its final form are controlled by the medium.

Media relations involves understanding the needs of the media you wish to deal with and meeting those needs. It includes meeting deadlines, making your news releases newsworthy and easy to use, and maintaining good relationships with reporters, editors and news directors.

Every organization has numerous "publics." To figure out who your "publics" are, think about who has a role in helping your organization achieve its goals and objectives.

The most obvious "public" or target audience for public relations is the customer or prospect. But there are many others who play roles in your success: suppliers, strategic partners, resellers, integrators, venture capitalists, bankers, end users, educators, competitors, investors, employees and their families, and the community in which you do business, as examples.

Even if you have a tightly defined customer market for your products and services, don't underestimate the importance of raising awareness of your company and your products and services within each of your target audiences.

Public relations can take many forms, for example:

PR can highlight new or improved products and services and promote them to customers or potential customers.

— It can announce changes within your organization.

— It can be informative and instructive.

— It can address industry issues and offer your company's position.

— It can highlight applications and the successes of your customers.

— It can inform the industry and the business community of alliances and strategic decisions.

— It can acknowledge and promote the local interests of your workforce.

— It can spark interest among potential investors or provide assurance to bankers, investors, and business partners you already have.

Let's examine the roles of these "publics" in assuring your company's success.

Customers buy your products and create cash flow for your company. Making and keeping customers is your ultimate reason for being in business.

The larger business community and others in your industry are attuned to changes in your organizational structure and in new hires. Key personnel changes or structural realignments can signal the direction your company is taking, its growth status, and its position in the industry. Attracting new talent to your company is a statement of achievement and stability and reflects your strategic planning. Name recognition can also spark a desire on the part of investors and prospects to investigate your company or look at it anew.

Likewise, the strategic alliances and partnerships you forge can tell your publics a lot about the strength and direction of your company and can attract investors, customers, and other potential partners.

Informative PR can help educate your many publics about the kind of business you are in, the issues your company or industry niche are dealing with, technological innovations, applications for your product or service, and your company's or product's position in the marketplace. It can also correct misapprehensions about your company or business and get your side of an issue before your publics in a positive way.

Your customers may appreciate being highlighted in a broader industry venue or to have a particular element of their operations receive recognition. For example, a hospital's IT department might not get much attention in the traditional medical press, but its innovations can be applauded in a specialty IT industry forum. This reflects well on the hospital and its employees and on you.

Employees like to see the company they work for headlined in local or industry media. It fosters pride and helps them feel a part of their local community and the industry. Raising awareness of your company in the community means when the employee says, "I work for XYZ Corporation," their friends and families have an idea what that means. Being known as a good place to work is a valuable commodity.

PR in the communities in which you do business positions your company as a good corporate citizen. People like to do business with others who share their interests and concerns and those who give back to the communities in which they operate. Employees also take pride in working for companies that support their communities. It's a wining situation and one that your company can justifiably take pride in and talk about.

So don't think of PR as simply a way to push your product or service. Strategic PR is a versatile, flexible, and creative tool to package and deliver your company's well-defined and managed message to your many audiences.

Media Advocacy and Public Health

Advocacy is used to promote an issue in order to influence policy-makers and encourage social change. Advocacy in public health plays a role in educating the public, swaying public opinion or influencing policy-makers.

Media coverage is one of the best ways to gain the attention of decision-makers. All monitor the media. Every staff person who monitors the news in the district or state and clips articles that mention the representative or senator by name. These articles are circulated to staff each week. Decisions to support legislative initiatives are frequently influenced by the media coverage.

Getting media coverage can be very easy. Public health advocate can reach thousands of other citizens, including policy-makers and their staff. Investing just a little more time can lead to significant payoffs for public health. You can also use the media to publicize community or state level pubic health events. Any meeting merits mention in the local newspaper's community calendar, and a workshop or a meeting with an outside speaker may warrant an article as well. Use each of these events to contact local reporters, editorial boards and radio and television talk show hosts. They may want to cover your event, and even if they do not, they will look to you as a resource person when they write about these issues in the future.

"Public health is what we, as a society, do collectively to assure the conditions in which people can be healthy." Before you can begin your advocacy, you need to have a plan. You need to know what the message is that you are trying to get across and you need to know any actions you want to be taken by the public, by other organizations or by legislators. First, you should establish what your overall goal is. Are you trying to motivate the community to take action on an issue? Are you advocating for a policy or law? Or are you just trying to bring attention to a certain issue? It is important that you have an overall goal before you start so that you can target your audience through the use of the media.

Here are some questions to ask yourself when developing your overall strategy. É_What is the problem you are highlighting? - This could be underage drinking, tobacco use, etc. But you should narrow your problem to a specific population. For example, if you start out trying to end all cigarette smoking, you will have a hard time developing a solution and gaining support. But if you narrow it down to underage smoking, you will have an easier time of coming up with a solution.

If you are trying to combat underage smoking, you could advocate for stricter laws for those who sell tobacco to minors. Do you want to use the media to get your message out by holding a news conference or briefing? Or do you want to use advertising to get the attention of the public? Remember, not all advocacy requires the use of the media. Sometimes it is easier to get your message out through marketing and advertising than through news releases and conferences.

Once you have defined your overall goal, then you can design the message that you want to get out in the public. You want your message to be simple and clear. You should point out the problem you are addressing, why your intended audience should be concerned with this problem and what should be done about the problem. Make your message powerful - persuasive and compelling. You will need to say something compelling to capture the attention of the public. Try to create a message that is new and put a human face on it. By humanizing the issue, your issues will have a greater impact on the public than if you just state statistics. Finally, make sure your message targets your intended audience. If you're targeting lawmakers, you will use different language than if you're trying to target the general community.

Contacting the Media

Before you begin to contact the media in your area, you should familiarize yourself with the local media. Watch the evening broadcasts and read the paper daily to get a feeling for how different stations and papers cover public health issues. This will give you an idea of who would be most likely to cover your story. Find out which reporters cover public health and track them to see how they cover the issues and if this is the type of reporter you would want to cover your story. It is also important to think about the audience that the station/paper reaches. You want to make sure that you use the best outlet to reach your intended audience.

If you want to mobilize the community, look at a local paper whose readers are mainly in the community you are trying to reach. If you are trying to get the attention of legislators, you may want to find a paper that covers politics and reaches a broader audience. If you want to send a message to your peers, you may want to try a trade magazine (i.e. Non-Profit Times, Healthcare Business Magazine).

Once you know what papers or stations you want to reach, you should create a list of media contacts. This list is perhaps the most important tool for conducting media advocacy. Developing such a list takes time, and it should continuously evolve. You need to get contact information. You will need the names of reporters, editors or producers, their address, phone numbers, fax numbers and e-mail addresses so that you will be able to send them your information in the format most appropriate for the type of story. Keep all of this information for future reference. To get this information, call the station or paper and ask. You can find out who covers a certain beat (a reporter's "beat" is the issue area he or she covers on a regular basis). If you are not sure with whom you need to talk, you can ask to speak to the news or assignment editor. This is the editor who assigns articles to the reporters and could help send you in the right direction.

Phone numbers for newspapers, radio and television stations are usually listed in the phonebook. You will need the number of the news desk and once you have that, you can call and get the information you need. Keep media sign-in sheets from any news events you hold and keep a log of all contacts you make with the media. Update your list with new contacts. This will keep you up-to-date on who covers which beat so that you will always have that information at your fingertips.

Finally, remember to create a good working relationship with the media. It will work to your advantage if you have a few "friends" in the media. That way, when you are contacting the media, you know that you have a few reporters you can rely on. This will make it easier than trying to contact everyone on your list. One well-placed, comprehensive story told from your organization's point-of-view, has a greater impact than a smattering of brief stories that don't adequately convey your message.

Before Making Contact With the Media

Once you have your message ready and know whom you want to contact in the media, take some time to prepare before you contact anyone. Divide up responsibility in your office, or have volunteers help out. You can divide up responsibility according to talent: designate one person to do any writing that needs to be done, have one person act as spokesperson, etc. This will make the workload lighter.

When choosing a spokesperson, make sure the person you choose is comfortable speaking with the media, answering questions, is knowledgeable on the issue and can stay calm in stressful situations. Dealing with the media can be very frustrating and fastpaced so it is important that your spokesperson be able to remain calm in these situations. Also, designate certain people on your staff who will speak with the media. They should be the only people to communicate with the press. This way, the media will not get conflicting information from your staff, but the planned message you are trying to get across.

Remember, know the message you are trying to get across and know your information before you speak to the media. Reporters work on deadline and need to get accurate information from you in a timely manner. If a reporter makes contact with you, you do not have to speak to them right away, but may want to take a message and call them back once you are prepared to speak to them. But remember to ask when their deadline is and call back promptly. If you call back after deadline, you may have missed your chance to get your story out.

Ways of Using the Media

There are many different ways you can use the media in advocacy. You can hold news conferences, write letters to the editor, give interviews or arrange editorial board meetings. The method you choose should be the best one to promote your issue.

News Release

Many reporters gather information for upcoming stories from news releases. The news release tells the reporter the who, what, when, where and why of a news story. This information helps the reporter determine whether to write an article or otherwise cover your "news." But remember, reporters receive many news releases over the week, so in order to get yours noticed, your release should quickly grab the reporter or editor's attention and the rest should convince him or her of the issue's news value. News releases generally follow a standard format. The format is designed to give the reporter or editor all the information he or she needs quickly. By following the same format, all pertinent information, such as contact information, is in the same place and easy for the reporter to find.

The following is the standard format for a news release:

Organization's name. The name of your organization should run across the top of the release. The release should be run on organizational letterhead if possible.

Contact information. Below the name of your organization, you need to put the name and phone/fax number and/or e-mail address of the staff person the press should contact to get more information. This is usually located on the top right-hand corner.

Release date. This tells the reporter when the information in the release can be published or broadcast. The release can be for immediate release to the public, in which you can put "For immediate release" on the top. The reporters can also hold the information until a certain date. For this, you would need to put "Embargoed until (release date and/or time)." The release date is usually located on the top left-hand corner.

Headline. The headline is important. It is a short phrase summing up the essence of the release. This will run under the contact information and above the body of the release.

Body. This is where you will tell the reporter/editor the who, what, where, when and why of your story.

Your release should follow the inverted pyramid style of writing, in which the conclusion or most important information goes first, followed by supporting information. This style of writing is necessary for any news materials because your readers are busy and bombarded with many different pieces of news. You can't count on the reader to get through the entire page so you must give the most important information - the essentials of the story - at the start.

Keep your sentences and paragraphs short and use plain language. Don't use acronyms or jargon. Also, you should try to keep your release short, one or two pages double-spaced should suffice.

Use quotes if possible. This puts a human face on the news you write. The quote should substantiate the lead, be from a significant person and add a piece of information. Try to put a quote high in the release, within the first three or four paragraphs.

Finish your release with a "tag." This is usually one paragraph of "boiler plate" information to fill in information holes such as a paragraph description of APHA, your organization or the goals of the work you've highlighted in the release.

End. Reporters/editors look for a symbol at the end of the release to tell them there is no more information. If your release is more than one page, at the end of the first page, type -more- to signal the release continues on the next page. News releases can be mailed, faxed or e-mailed to reporters. You may want to call the reporter to make sure that he or she has received your release or that the right reporter has it. Remember, reporters are often busy meeting deadlines so make your call brief and to the point.

Letter to the Editor

A letter to the editor is the simplest way to communicate an opinion to the general public. The chances of having the letter printed greatly increases at smaller or less prominent newspapers or magazines. The most important caveat is to write a letter no longer than what the target newspaper tends to publish. A much longer letter is more likely to be discarded, and if it is not discarded, it is the editor who will decide what information will be cut in order to fit the length requirements. Short, pithy pieces are best.

Before you begin writing your letter, look at the editorial pages of different newspapers. Often, specifications on writing letters to the editor will be on this page. If not, follow these general tips for writing your letter.

— *Be brief and concise.* Focus your letter on just one concept or idea. Limit yourself to 250-300 words.

— *Refer to other stories.* If possible, refer to other articles, editorials or letters the newspaper has recently published. This should be done as soon as possible after the article was published. This will increase its chances of being printed.

— *Include contact information.* Include your name, address and daytime and home phone number so the paper can contact you with any questions. Also, include any titles and degrees that are relevant to help the media know you have expertise. And make sure to refer to your organization in your letter.

Op-ed

Another way of contacting the media is by writing an opinion piece to be run on a newspaper's opinion-editorial page. Writing an opinion article offers an opportunity to present an extended argument. They run on the page opposite the newspaper's editorials and are typically local and timely. Unlike editorials, op-eds are written by members of the community rather than by journalists. But like editorials, an op-ed often carries more weight than a letter to the editor; it presents a point of view with much greater detail and persuasion than a short letter allows.

Careful planning will increase your chances of placing an op-ed. In addition to submitting an article, mount a campaign to get it published. Be sure to follow up within a week after submitting an article to ensure that it was received and to answer questions the editor might have. Before you submit your op-ed, you will want to:

Obtain guidelines. Call and ask the editorial page editor or op-ed editor for the newspaper's op-ed policies, i.e., submission guidelines such as length (usually 700-800 words).

Talk to the editor. Try to arrange an appointment with the editorial staff to discuss your unique qualifications for writing an op-ed and the issue's urgency. Use the meeting to sell your issue, your organization and yourself. Some newspapers will not take time to meet with you; they will make a decision based solely on the article. At the very least, the editor might have useful suggestions on how to write your article and improve its chances of being published.

Localize it. Adopt a local angle in your op-ed, even on a national issue. Since you're probably competing for space with nationally syndicated columnists, a local angle can make your article more appealing.

Most papers require exclusivity; you may only submit your op-ed to their publication. If they decline to print it, you are free to submit the piece to another publication.

Editorial Board Meeting

The most powerful way to win support for your issue or local official through the media is to gain the editorial support of your newspaper. Arranging an editorial board meeting will take more time than writing a letter to the editor, but the results are worth the effort. This will give you the chance to persuade the editor why the newspaper's readers would be interested in your story and this could increase the likelihood of more coverage by the newspaper of your issue.

Here are some tips on arranging a meeting:

Call the editorial page editor. Briefly explain the issue and request a meeting. It is best if the issue is tied to a particular news event or local concern.

Prepare for the meeting. Study the issue, write down key facts and list your main points. Think through the local angle. Why should your community or the newspaper's readers - and the editor - care about the issue? It might also help to familiarize yourself with the kinds of editorials and columns that appear in the paper. This will give you insight into the paper's position on certain issues.

Present your issue. You might meet with one editor, or perhaps several editorial writers and reporters will decide to join your meeting. You will have five or 10 minutes to state your case as persuasively as possible, after which you will be asked questions. If you do not know the answers, offer to find out and get back to the editor later.

Follow up. Leave behind some printed material reinforcing the points you have made. After the meeting, send a note of thanks to the editor. If you do not see an editorial within a few days, make a follow-up phone call to the editor. If the editor has decided not to write on your issue, ask if the paper would print an op-ed or at least a letter to the editor submitted by you. Whatever you achieve, you have established yourself and APHA as a source of information on public health issues in your community.

Interview

Another way of working with the media is to give interviews. There are more than 10,000 television and radio stations nationwide, each with producers constantly on the lookout for story ideas and guests to have on their shows. Local talk shows have also become a significant force in national politics.

Following are some tips to help you arrange and prepare for an interview.

Arrange an appearance. Call or write the talk show host or producer. Explain your interest and experience in a particular aspect of public health, and outline why people in your community should care. Again, it is best to have an upcoming event or a local angle as a "news peg" to make your pitch more attractive.

Familiarize yourself with the program. Learn the name of the host, the show, the station and names of other guests appearing on your program. Find out whether the interview will be live or taped, if there will be call-in questions and the length of the interview. Listen to the program to become familiar with the style and positions of the host and the format of the show.

Prepare for the interview. Write out the most important points you hope to make, including anecdotes and personal stories you want to share, questions you might anticipate and answers to those questions. Role-play answering those questions with a partner. Also, you may want to think out some counter-arguments to your issue and prepare responses to them. Remember that the media usually presents both sides of a story so you want to be able to counter your opponents' viewpoints. When being interviewed, there are several things to keep in mind to help make the interview go smoothly.

Speak in a natural, audible tone. Remember to remain calm during the interview, even during stressful moments. Do not get defensive or angry. Keep in mind that the reporter decides what goes in the story or what doesn't, so you don't want to say anything that you would not want to see on the evening news.

Avoid jargon and acronyms. Remember, not everyone is an expert on your issue. You should use language that will be easily understood by someone outside of your field of expertise.

State your message. Answer interview questions by stating your main message first, followed by supporting points. Use the questions as springboards into developing your message. Present your arguments as concisely as possible while showing enthusiasm for your subject. If you don't know the answer to a question, say so. Also, don't be afraid to speak up if the reporter misstates something or has a wrong fact.

Be concise. It is important to keep your answers short, especially in broadcast interviews. Soundbites in broadcast interviews usually run around eight seconds long, so you want to get your message out quickly. Print reporters also look for concise quotes for their stories. Say what you have to say then wait for the next question. Don't feel compelled to fill "dead air" while waiting for the next question. Some reporters may wait a beat before asking another question, hoping you will jump in and fill the silence. This often results in remarks being made that you wouldn't normally want on the record.

Tape yourself. You may want to bring along a tape recorder to make your own record of what was said in the interview. This way, if there is an error or misquote in the story, you will have your own record of what was actually said. Make sure that everyone involved in the interview knows you are taping it. When being interviewed for television, there are several additional things to remember.

Clothing. Avoid solid white or black clothing and anything with tight stripes. Solid designs in gray, blue and brown look best. Avoid large, flashy jewelry. Large jewelry will create a reflection off the TV lights. Dress professionally. If you wear a uniform to work (lab coat, military, etc.) consider wearing that for your interview.

Look at the interviewer. Unless otherwise instructed, look directly at the host. Do not look at the camera. Relax and avoid nervous gestures or mannerisms. Use, but do not overuse, your smile and hand gestures.

Sit straight. You want to sit up straight, but not stiff, and lean slightly forward in your chair. Do not lean into the microphone. Avoid swiveling in your chair. If standing, stand up straight. Do not place feet side to side, but plant more weight on one foot. This will keep you from swaying.

You're always "on." Remember, even if you are not speaking, you may still be on camera. And any comments you make prior to or after the formal interview may be caught on camera or tape, so mind your actions.

After the interview, follow up with a note of thanks to the reporter, host or producer of the program. You can often request a taped copy or written transcript of the program for your files. If you provide a videocassette or audiocassette prior to the program, they may make a tape for you. Listen and learn for your next on-air experience. If there is an error in the story, contact the reporter and point out the error and ask for a correction. But remember to remain calm. Also, try to go directly to the reporter to fix the error instead of going over his or her head to the editor or producer. Doing this should only be done if there is a major mistake and the reporter will not acknowledge it. By going over the reporter's head, you may ruin any working relationship you had developed, so this step should only be done in extreme circumstances.

Media Event

In some cases, you may want to consider holding a media event to disseminate your information. The two most common media events are the press briefing and news conference.

A press briefing is held to provide journalists with background information on an issue. A briefing is a good way to provide journalists with an update of key developments and issues, as well as your organization's work and policy, on a certain topic. These meetings can be informal and are a good way to make contacts with the media. A news conference is held to announce a major story - such as the release of a report, a new policy that has been developed or your organization is taking a new major initiative on an issue.

Press briefings and news conferences are major undertakings and require a lot of work and preparation. But they can be very valuable when you have important information to release, a critical situation has developed, an important speaker has become available or you have a dramatic point of presentation to make on an important issue. Most often, contacting reporters individually or holding a briefing for a small group is a better use of time and resources. But on occasion, you may need to hold a news conference to draw attention to a particular public health issue.

While such an event takes preparation and a lot of legwork, one committed person or a small group sharing the work can undertake it. Consider dividing up the work among your staff to make it easier. Following are a few suggestions for planning and holding a media event.

Location. You will want to find a well-known location that is convenient for journalists to get to. Make sure the room is not too large. This way there won't be a lot of empty seats, giving the impression that few journalists showed up. Also, make sure there is a podium and a table long enough for all of the speakers to sit at. There should also be adequate open space for television cameras, lights and microphones. Usually, television cameras will be placed in the back of the room so there should be plenty of open space in the back. The room should also have plenty of electrical outlets. Popular sites for media events include hotels, local press clubs or public buildings near media offices. Also appropriate is using a location that highlights public health as a backdrop for your issue, i.e., a local health department, a children's hospital, a school or a community park.

Timing. Journalists have very busy schedules so timing is important. The best time to hold an event is around 10 a.m. or 11 a.m. on a Tuesday, Wednesday or Thursday. Plan around competing events, holidays or other activities that may impede journalists from attending your event.

Contacting the media. Send a media advisory several days to a week in advance if you have the luxury of time. If not, e-mail and fax the advisory. Include in the media advisory the location, time and date of the event, with brief directions if necessary, the names of speakers and an eye-catching summary of the presentation. Follow up with phone calls to the journalists several days later. Call a day or two before the news conference to draw their attention to the release and ask if they or someone from their office plan to attend. This is critical. Newsrooms are swamped with releases, faxes and invitations to events. A follow-up phone call will ensure that your contacts know about the event and remember to put it on their calendars.

Materials. You will want to have material at your press event to give out to the media. The easiest way to hand out material is to put together a press kit. A press kit usually contains news releases, fact sheets and biographies of speakers as well as copies of any reports, case studies, etc., that are being released at the event. Make sure you have plenty of copies of all material with you in case more people attend than planned for. Also, have a sign-in sheet for any journalists attending. Remember to use this sheet to add to and update your media contact list.

Prepare. Set up the room for the number of people that you invited. Don't be disappointed if fewer people showed up than expected. Attendance is hard to predict. Your event may be competing against another news event. Select a moderator for the event. Determine beforehand who will make opening remarks, introduce each speaker and direct questions following the presentation.

Resource people. Have extra people from your staff available to assist at the event. You will need someone to assist journalists before and during the conference. Have some help in handing out media kits, managing the sign-in sheet, directing journalists to phones or handle any other last minute details.

Presenting. Make your formal statement as brief as possible - 15 or 20 minutes -while still getting in all the pertinent information and allow time for questions. A general rule of thumb is to limit the number of speakers to no more than five and limit each speaker to three to five minutes. Remember, a news conference is for the media to ask questions, not attend a lecture. Also, start your event on time. Journalists work on deadlines and will need plenty of time to get your story in before deadline.

Interviews. Allow time at the conclusion of the event to take personal interviews, arrange photos or answer more detailed questions.

Follow up. After the event, thank reporters for attending and ask if they need any further information. You may also want to fax or e-mail material to those journalists who were unable to attend. Also, make sure your staff knows who to direct phone calls to from journalists calling for follow-up.

Feedback. Respond in writing to any news stories your event or media outreach garners. Reporters pay attention to response letters - both positive and negative - and will often integrate the comments into future stories.

9

Modern Approach to Public Relations

Modern public relations practitioners are facing more difficulties and challenges as information speed and globalization alter the pace and landscape of the profession. Modern business, characterized by globalization, requires organizations to understand the intercultural and international aspects of public relations while operating in a global market. The internationalization of public relations is both an opportunity and a challenge for professionals. Understanding the traditional social culture might still be one of the most difficult challenges for public relations practitioners working in international contexts.

International public relations would have to reflect the cultural and societal norms of the host nation. Cultural variation, different norms of conduct, and different levels of social-political development all will demand different approaches to the practice. In addition to cultural challenges, public relations practitioners are facing technological challenges as well. The days when press releases served as the primary tool for public relations practitioners have long passed. Instead, Internet, digital technology and e-commerce present technological challenges that significantly alter modern public relations.

In fact, websites are quickly becoming a widely adopted public relations tool. While organizations, ranging from production to service to technology, are adopting websites, public relations are a particularly important consideration for organizations as they begin to serve their various constituencies through the Web. Public relations have demonstrated to be especially vital for banks given the extremely competitive banking environment. As Morvis identified, Banks must integrate public relations into the decision-making and business planning process if they wish to deflect rising public concern over the financial stability of the industry. Effective issues management, corporate identity protection, and systematic crisis communications are key strategies, which can be used to defend a banking institutions credibility before negative publicity weakens its reputation.

J. Grunig identified the two-way symmetrical model as a way of practicing public relations through "using bargaining, negotiating, and strategies of conflict resolution to bring about symbiotic changes in the ideas, attitudes, and behaviours of both the organization and its publics. It is this two-way symmetrical model, which is characterized as most ethical and effective in practice, which provides a normative theory for achieving excellent communication management. Thus, Grunig regards the two-way symmetrical model as excellent public relations. A prominent theme in public relations research and commentary since the articulation of Grunigs model has focused on "either supporting or challenging James Grunigs symmetrical model of public relations as most ethical way to conduct public relations. The significance of the two-way symmetrical model can be found from the following two aspects.

First, the two-way symmetrical model makes organizations more effective. From a directional perspective, two-way communication, such as two-way symmetrical model, allows for the exchange of information - information flows freely between systems, such as organizations, publics, managements, and employees. From a purposive perspective, symmetrical communication, seeks moving equilibrium through cooperation and mutual adjustment. In contrast, asymmetrical communication "leaves the organization as is and tries to change the public. It can be generalized that organizations will become much more effective through two-way symmetrical public relations than through one-way communication or asymmetrical positions.

Grunig presents several reasons why a two-way symmetrical relationship is best including

(1) there are no clear boundaries between organizations and other systems due to free flow of information;

(2) conflicts will be resolved through negotiation and communication due to thoughts of cooperation and mutual benefits; and

(3) the input of all people, including employees, is valued.

Second, the two-way symmetrical model makes organizational public relations more ethical. As Lindeborg argues, two-way symmetrical public relations "serve as a mechanism by which organizations and publics interact to manage interdependence and conflict for the benefit of all. It implies that everyone involved is equal. Everything can be solved through dialogue, discussion and negotiation. By promoting bonds of mutual trust between the organization and its publics by empowering them to shape and collaborate on organizational goals through feedback, the organization-public relationship is strengthened. On the contrary, the other three models, press agentry / publicity, public information, two-way asymmetrical, tend to be less ethical.

As Grunig and Hunt proposed, the press agentry / publicity model is dominated by one-way, persuasive communication aimed at manipulating audience attitudes and behaviours, while the public information practitioner provides accurate information about her or his organization to the public but does not volunteer negative information. These two models established communication as one-directional, from organization to public. Although the emergence of the two-way asymmetrical model shifted communication from one-way to two-way, which significantly altered communication relationship; the primary goal for feedback under this model is to refine persuasive message strategies toward specific targeted publics in an effort to predict behaviour.

The personal influence model, known as the fifth model of public relations has been shown as prevalent in Far Eastern countries. In this model, interpersonal communication is argued to play a large persuasive role in attitude. In many nations in the developing world, organizations tend to ignore the attitudes of mass publics and instead focus specifically on the attitudes of journalists and government officials. Thus, the personal influence is a "pervasive public relations technique.

Furthermore, Taylor suggested "Practitioners traveling to countries with hierarchical cultures should keep this in mind when developing public relations strategies. For example, the hierarchically-structured Chinese culture represents a model for public relations practitioners to conduct the personal influence public relations. Culbertson and Chen, through interviewing with Chinese female public relations practitioners, found that the achievement of many professional, personal, and social goals rests on a concept of gao guanxi, which means "establishing connections, creating obligations and favours among interactants, and enjoying privileges through relationships.

Performing the gao guanxi role in the Chinese society has an instructive purpose of helping practitioners to identify key publics. Taylor and Kent found that "multiple publics may be an important part of public relations communication in the developed world, but in the developing world, specific publics such as journalists and government officials may actually be more important publics. Specifically, "the offices of government are the key publics. Therefore, "government becomes the target of most public relations efforts, rather than the source of them. Thus, public relations practice in various cultures demands that practitioners understand the very real cultural differences as well as the structural obstacles that challenge their goal of reaching target publics.

Culture Variation

The term culture has many definitions. Kroeber and Kluckhohn analyzed 160 definitions of the concept of "culture." After their analysis, Kroeber and Kluckhohn presented a definition of culture they felt encompassed the way scholars have operationalized culture as follows:

> Culture consists of patterns, explicit and implicit, of and for behaviour acquired and transmitted by symbols, constituting the distinctive achievements of human groups, including their embodiments in artifacts; the essential core of culture consists of traditional (i.e., historically derived and selected) ideas and especially their attached values; culture systems may, on the one

> hand, be considered as products of action, on the other as conditioning elements of further action.

Obviously, culture is one of the most complicated but more influential factors that guide human behaviour and human thoughts. As Kim and Gudykunst noted, "we say persons belong to a similar culture, we are saying they share certain psychological, sociological, and technological trappings. Thus, in the area of public relations practice, as many researchers propose, culture influences the practice of public relations in every nation and region of the world. Geetz Hofstede proposed one of the hallmark theories about culture, in which he defined culture as "the collective programming of the mind which distinguishes the members of one human group from another.

Culture in this sense, included systems of values; and values are among the building blocks of culture. Furthermore, Hofstede extensively observed culture in the workplace and identified four dimensions of culture - collectivism/individualism, masculinity/femininity, uncertainty avoidance, and power distance, which "offer a means to examine practices in different cultures.

Individualism versus Collectivism

Hofstede defined individualism versus collectivism as one of the four dimensions of culture. Furthermore, Hui and Triandis conducted a survey of cross-cultural anthropologists and psychologists from all parts of the world and concluded, "the dimension of individualism - collectivism can be used as a powerful theoretical construct to explain the degree of international differences and similarities between cultures. Given the differences between individualism and collectivism in definition, the countries which embedded either in individualism or collectivism will value human thoughts, behaviours, beliefs, and even the social norms in entirely different ways. Hofstede found out that the United States and China are the representatives on the either side of the individualism versus collectivism index.

Specifically, the US has the individualistic culture, whereas China is a country of the collectivistic culture. Some other empirical studies have provided the evidence that there are four major differences between individualism and the collectivism. First, both cultures define the "self differently. The individualistic culture, such as the US culture, defines the self as "an autonomous entity, independent of groups whereas the collectivistic culture, such as the Chinese culture, defines the self in terms of its connectedness to others in various in-groups.

Second, both cultures define personal goals in different ways. The individualistic US culture views the personal goals prior to the group goals, whereas the collectivistic Chinese culture regards the personal goals as a subordinate to the group goals. Third, both cultures define social behaviour differently. Individualistic culture believes that social behaviour is more likely to be driven by their own beliefs, values, and attitude; whereas the collectivistic culture proposes that social behaviours are more likely to be driven by social norms, duties, and obligations.

Finally, both cultures weigh relationships differently. The individualistic culture is more oriented toward task achievement, sometimes at the expense of relationships, whereas the collectivistic culture emphasizes harmonious relationships, sometimes at the expense of task accomplishment. And these differences will definitely affect communication in the workplace.

Chinese culture is influenced greatly by Confucianism, the philosophy named after the Chinese philosopher Confucius of 500 BC. The key point of Confucianism is that it is a philosophy of human nature that considers proper relationships as the basis of the society. Specifically, Redding and Wong suggested four traits consistent with Confucian ideology that have "significant impact on present day organizations in overseas Chinese.

These traits are as follows:

1. Socialization within the family unit in such a way as to promote sobriety, education, the acquisition of skills, and seriousness about tasks, job, family, and obligations.
2. A tendency to help the group (however it might be identified).
3. A sense of hierarchy and of its naturalness and rightness
4. A sense of complementarities in relationship, which combined, with the sense of hierarchy, enhances perceptions of fairness and equity in institutions.

Based upon these four traits, Hwang defined the Chinese society as "relational orientation." Given the fact that relational orientation plays important roles, traditional Chinese decide their relationships with others from two aspects: relationship hierarchy and relationship closeness. First, as Huang identified, the Chinese society is hierarchically structured and the basic relations follow an asymmetrical norm. There are five basic relations in Chinese society - sovereign and subordinate, father and son, elder brother and younger brother, spouse and spouse, and friend and friend.

In each pair, the latter one will subordinate to the former one, the former is superior to the latter one. It is basically a priority-subordination relation. "To a Confucian, all human relationships in the society can be derived from one or combination of these five fundamental relationships. For example, a teacher-student relationship in China is usually perceived as a father-son relationship. Bond and Hwang found that Confucianism, which emphasizes hierarchical authority and justifies the unequal distribution of power and wealth, has been the "major and most powerful source of legitimacy for the upper classes to rule Chinese society.

Furthermore, "The paternal authoritarian culture has developed a superior-subordinate bureaucracy where the paramount leader is the centre of the power. The patriarchal nature of Chinese banking industry is a good example that depicts the asymmetric relationships among Chinese. The public considers the banks president as the sovereign. What the president says to the public will be viewed as authority or power, and will not be challenged on merit or value.

For instance, in the first half-year of 1999, both China Construction Bank (CCB) and Bank of China (BOC) were planning to conduct individual buying and selling of foreign exchange. In order to compete with BOC, which was known as the top one to manage China's foreign exchange and to conduct international payments, the CCB carried out a series of promotions. One of the promotions was that the president of CCB addressed the publics on television, whereas BOC issued news releases for newspapers. Consequently, CCB won more customers than BOC.

Later on, a survey showed that there was a high correlation between the presidents television address and the reason why the public chose CCB as their bank.

Second, with respect to the extent of relationship closeness, Hwangs model of face and favour-"the means that people use the most in this tie to expand their human network and obtain resources from resource allocates — provides a clear picture. Specifically, the face and favour model categorized human relationship into three types on the basis of their expressive and instrumental components.

The first category is expressive tie, and the most important expressive tie in Chinese society is the relationship between members in a family or other congenial groups. The second tie, mixed tie, characterizes the relationship outside an individual's immediate family. The third category is instrumental ties. In this category, an individual establishes temporary and anonymous relationships with people, such as customers, salesperson, taxi drivers, and so forth.

Obviously, these three categories of social ties in Chinese society briefly delineate the basic relationships among the Chinese. The people will behave based on identifying which tie they have with each other. Basically, the face and favour model of social ties has provided a positive framework for daily public relations practices. However, there are downsides as well when the face and favour model is over emphasized by public relations practitioners.

First, the clear and stereotyped relationship in Chinese society helps public relations practitioners identify and understand relationships among the public, the organization, and the media. According to Hwang's idea, the relationship between an individual customer and a bank is usually categorized as an instrumental tie. The relationship between the customer and the bank in this stage is supposed to be very loose. However, the strong competition makes the organization have to think about how to strategically win customers and the competition ultimately.

Strategically, a bank should attempt to engage into other tighter ties, such as the mixed tie and the expressive tie, because when a Chinese perceives himself or herself to be in such situations, the notions of "loyalty, obedience, respect, and service will be expected in these ties. Although the task is even harder for American public relations practitioners in the Chinese society, they have ways to solve this problem. Huang notes, "Confucianism provides human beings with a society in which people can quickly recognize the reality (the specific relationship with certain others) and can easily adapt themselves to their changing environment".

This relational issue is even harder for the public relations practitioners of the US banks in China for two reasons. First, the notion of "relational orientation" in Chinese society is alien in the US. The Chinese consider man as a relational being, "socially situated and defined within an interactive context"; whereas the Americans see man as an independent individual. Such fundamentally different viewpoints of human definitely influence the practice conducted by the public relations practitioners of the US banks in China.

Second, those public relations practitioners of the US banks in China will encounter the conflicts of ethical issues. The way that most Chinese conduct public relations based upon the personal influence model, which is more common in China, will not appear to be ethical to the US public relations practitioners. The fact that public relations practitioners take advantage of personal relations causes the ethical problems in terms of the Western view. Therefore, the social ties are to some extent negative toward the public relations practices in the real setting.

Banking Environment

Ever since the economic reform began in 1978, the banking sector has undergone great changes, both in the infrastructure of banking system and the business scope. The addition of foreign banks operating in China has enhanced such changes since the mid 1980s.

Except for the central bank - Peoples Bank of China, there are two tiers of all the commercial banks in China. The first tier is usually referred to the Big Four - Industrial and Commercial Bank, Agricultural Bank, Bank of China, and China Construction Bank. These four most important state-owned commercial banks control 70% of all financial assets in China with a total of 1.6 million workers. To some extent, these "Big Four have no competitors in terms of their priority and long-standing honour in the public. The bulk of outstanding loans in China belong to the "Big Four state banks. When restrictions on foreign banks are presented later, the central banks set those strict rules, mainly to protect the domestic banks. Despite foreign bank presence, the Big Four are still the major players in Chinas banking environment, particularly because they have the government on their side.

A second tier of commercial banks has emerged since the early 1990s, which has provided new banking models for consumers. The four famous commercial banks are Shanghai Pudong Development Bank (SPDB), China Communication Bank (CCB), China Minsheng Banking Corporation Limited, and China Everbright Bank. These banks squeezed into the banking market with the sponsor of a state institute. In many ways, these new banks are more efficient than the Big Four and offer a much better quality of service. Due to their highly-educated management groups, these commercial banks are modeled after the Western banking system.

Dai Xianglong, governor of the Peoples Bank of China, wants to "give banks freedom to set their own interest rates and let more of them to follow SPDB onto the stock market. The discussion on this second tier of commercial banks will contribute to the identification of opportunities for foreign banks. This new second tier of banks is competitive with foreign banks, because they are not under as much governmental restriction as the Big Four. Furthermore, they are comparable to Western banks in services they provide to their customers.

China opened the door to foreign banks in the early 1990s. Leung described the situation in which the foreign banks stepped into the China market as follows: Scarce capital has been allocated to relatively inefficient and loss-making state-owned enterprises (Sues), while small and medium-sized firms have often been denied the funds. At this juncture, foreign capital from or through international banks have bridged the gap between savings and investment. Foreign banks, entering China mainly to follow and serve their clients from home countries, have been restricted to foreign currency business - until recently.

There are three stages of foreign banks development since the Chinese government permitted foreign banks to enter the China market, and within each stage, foreign banks became less bounded. The first stage began in early eighties, during which the Chinese government allowed foreign banks to set up representative offices to engage in "liaison service in Beijing. Eight foreign banks, including Citibank, got the first operation licenses. The second stage began around the early 1990s. With the second boom of China economy after the 1978 reform, foreign banks started to gain more operational rights. First of all, foreign banks began to set up branches instead of representative offices.

As Leung noted, "a physical branch in China has emerged as the best 'institution for internalizing the countrys various advantage. Second, nearly all foreign banks in China have been allowed to provide loans only to joint ventures and engage in trade finance. Others beyond this scope were strictly prohibited. Foreign banks at that time still had no access right to local currency business. Although real changes were clear, the changes represent small steps in the banking environment.

The third stage is the most prosperous one among these three, symbolized by the 1997 more in which Peoples Bank of China permitted five foreign banks to do business in the local Renminbi (Renminbi-China currency) in China. Citibank NA, the Hong Kong and Shanghai Bank, the Bank of Tokyo-Mitsubishi, and the Industrial Bank of Japan became the first license holders. In March 1997, the New Pudong area of Shanghai was designated as the first location to allow foreign banks to engage in Rmb (Chinese currency) business, though on a very restricted basis. "[T] hose banks can undertake local currency business only with joint ventures in Shanghai, however; consumer banking with Chinese citizens is prohibited. By the end of 2000, 32 of the 178 foreign banks have local currency business licenses. Though some restrictions obviously were lifted, most of the foreign banks still "can only watch with envy as Chinese banks swoop in on foreign clients increasingly seeking yuan currency loans to avoid exchange rate risk and to pay lower rates.

The foreign banks in China have advantages in the competitive environment. First, the foreign banks in general have competitive edges in the areas of financial soundness, risk management, and financial innovations, which the Chinese government must consider when it attempts to balance the attraction of foreign banks with the protection of local banks. As Chowdhurys research on Citibank reveals, "As Chinese households realize that the foreign banks can provide better products and services, they start to take their money out of Chinese banks and put it in foreign ones. In terms of business operation, Chinese banks have few competitive capabilities with foreign banks to date.

Another big hope for foreign banks is Chinas accession to the World Trade Organization (WTO). Accession to the WTO will result in fewer restrictions for foreign banks. The market segmentation between domestic and foreign banks is to be gradually eliminated. "Foreign banks will be able to conduct Rmb business with Mainland firms and citizens in phases after Chinas WTO entry. Yet as Citigroup Chairman Sandy Weill acknowledges, the twin deadlines of 2002 (opening of the corporate market) and 2005 (opening of the retail market) will be critical to the banking environment in China.

Public Relations and Banking

Many studies reviewed how crucial public relations is to the banking industry. Although there are no specific studies conducted in the China banking market, the findings mostly reviewed through U.S. and Australia researchers offer much insight to the industry. As Morvis proposed, maintaining and communicating a strong corporate identity is now essential for successful banks. Today, banks have become more homogeneous in the public eye. Customers are more apt to change banks at a moments notice to get a better deal, better service or more conveniences. Thus, creating a reputable image means much more than developing a tag line to use behind the corporate name.

Traditionally, "Banks can enhance their image by publicizing their commitment to the community and their customers. Morvis also recognized that, todays banker is forced to defend his institutions fiscal strength as well as its credibility before customers, shareholders, employees and the community. One of the primary mechanisms banks use to accomplish credibility is through coordinating public relations. Since interest rates, the economy, and fiscal issues are prominent among citizens, media attention and handling of these issues is crucial to consumer confidence and spending choices.

Most bankers, therefore, seek communications strategies to help manage relations with the press and other critical publics. Merrick reviewed public relations within the banking industry from the perspective of the characteristics of banking. He proposed that "In the banking industry public relations is important, since the public has become more concerned about the safety of their investments and accounts. Furthermore, Merrick suggested that bank communicators should monitor newspaper articles and radio announcements for accuracy, since local media is the key to maintaining local support. A bank should also keep all of its employees informed. "This confidence crisis must be faced with absolutely honest public information.

In China, the concept of public relations is a new idea to most of Chinese banks. Previously there was no certain public relations division in banking structure. The China banking system consists of a central bank and the four big state-owned banks mentioned previously. These banks do not need to compete with each other since the central bank and the government have defined their business scope. Things changed a little in 1996, when the China Construction Bank (CCB) launched the first public relations department in its Beijing Branch in order to meet the requirements of its system reform -transforming into a commercial bank through establishing its new image. The success of the PR campaign of CCB intrigued many bankers and popularized public relations practice among banks in China.

However, although there is no certain public relations division in traditional banks in China, some of the PR jobs were allocated in other divisions. For instance, the Office of Secretaries typically is charged with delivering publications, while Foreign Affairs Department deals with the information exchanging with foreign customers or foreign cooperators. The primary functions of these departments centre on information-oriented public relations activities. On the surface, these functions look much like Grunigs public information model, which is characterized as one-way information delivery.

Most Chinese banks conduct their public relations practice this way due to their long history of centralization and exclusive priorities. However, with the competition enhanced, more banks are starting to observe their public, attempting to identify what customers really want, and how to cater to their needs. Public relations in Chinese banking will play a tremendous role in such a competitive and changing global context.

Public Relations and the Internet (Website)

As the Internet becomes a more dominant communication

medium, not only in the business industry, but also in individual communication, the field of public relations will inevitably be transformed. Many studies reviewed how important the Internet is towards the field of public relations, and why those public relations practitioners are adopting the Internet as a primary public relations medium in the modern age. All the studies done under the rubric of Internet and public relations focus on two major aspects: the form and function of the Internet as a public relations tool. It is important to review the technical, practical, and problematical issues these studies address as follows.

The first group of studies concentrated on why the Internet is becoming a popular public relations tool. As Hill and White identified, the World Wide Web is becoming a significant communications tool for businesses and organizations. They proposed, "Web sites are used to keep stakeholders up-to-date, provide information to the media, gather information about publics, strengthen corporate identity, and a host of other public relations functions. In fact, the three major entities in public relations -media, corporations, and publics - may be linked by the structural opportunities that websites provide. Certainly, these features, in addition to the relatively low cost, are reasons the Internet has developed so rapidly as a public relations tool, and should emerge as superior to other tools in the near future.

One of the fundamental challenges for public relations professionals is to ensure favourable media coverage and attention for their organizations goals. Traditionally in public relations, controlled messages are sent through newsletters, annual reports, and other vehicles that are written by communication professionals in an organization. Prior to the Internet, the only way to design these messages to meet specific customers or potential customers needs was through mass media or direct mail.

Media gatekeeping can significantly alter organization messages and an organizations ability to reach its targeted publics through mass media. Thus, advertising and direct mail, more expensive endeavours for organizations, are relied upon by many organizations. White and Raman noted the trend to use the web for public relations type activities. They contend, "the web is the first controlled public relations mass medium in that content reaches a mass audience, but is not filtered through gatekeepers. This less expensive form of controlled communication is a feature that will undoubtedly make the web a primary public relations tool.

However, using the website does not mean replacing all other kinds of traditional public relations tools. Instead, a website is seen as enhancing the performance of other public relations tools used by practitioners. The web provides visitors additional information or offers easy access to the organization. However, the use of modern technologies in public relations field is not well developed or well balanced either in practice or in research. A survey of public relations practitioners found that although the use of technology is identified as a leading public relations trend, its "impact and value are mixed. Furthermore, Johnson noted that rigorous public relations research about the use of new technologies has been limited.

The second group of studies focused on how public relations practitioners or professionals deploy the Internet technology in daily practices. As the study done by Cowlett identified, organizations like Shell and British Airways are pushing the Internet as a public relations tool. Shell launched its site in response to attacks over issues such as its controversial involvement in Nigeria. The site explains Shells stance on such sensitive issues and encourages both positive and negative feedback via e-mail and online discussion.

Another study by Hill and White identified the importance of e-mail used for public relations. They stated that the e-mail function is seen as offering two-way communication opportunities. Randy Bobbitt proposed that electronic mail, the World Wide Web (WWW), Usenet, ListServ, Gopher and TelNet are most beneficial features for PR professionals. He emphasized that, "e-mail can be used for intracompany or intradepartment communication, communication between agencies and clients, communication between PR professionals and media people, and interviews with spokespersons. In sum, e-mail is attractive because it can be used to provide information both to the internal and external publics.

Although public relations practitioners and researchers are highly in favour of the Internet as a new tool for practice, they still debate over the ability of the Internet to replace some traditional public relations tools. According to Hill and White, most people are suspect about the Internets ability to replace traditional public relations tools, such as a press release, a public service announcement, or a brochure. For instance, most organizations routinely post news releases to their sites without abandoning traditional methods of distributing releases. They did not think the audiences of their newsletters would visit the website to get the same information and did not believe the web replaced face-to-face communication.

The use of traditional public relations strategies are re-emerging in the UK, as companies return to traditional public relations to help mitigate the spread of misinformation on the Internet. Furthermore, Daniel Dern expressed "Dont think that the Internet can replace good PR people it cant. Thus, e-mail and the Web can help public relations departments transmit information to the press more quickly, but the Internet needs to be carefully managed as a public relations tool.

Based upon the research on public relations and the Internet, along with the evolving context of the banking environment in China, the research presented here aims to explore the websites of three banks operating in the Chinese market. The goal of the in-depth analysis of the websites is to explore questions regarding similarities and differences based on cultural features, dialogic features, and other design aspects that appear to position the organization to engage in two-way communication with its various publics.

Public relations with Chinese features, then, must develop in accordance with unique Chinese characteristics, which will result in the fact that "the basic philosophies, principles, roles, and functions of public relations in China would be expected to differ from those in the United States and other Western countries. There are three basic economic systems in China. They are Chinese state-owned, Chinese private-owned and foreign banks operating in the country. Due to the different social status, organizations with different economic systems perform differently in establishing relations with the various publics.

Impact of Internet

More than half a century ago, Harold D. Lasswell, a distinguished Yale University sociologist, suggested the scientific study of the process of communication could be narrowed down to an examination of, "Who says What to

Whom through which Channel with what Effect. " While this noted paradigm would be at the center of much of the communication study and research which took place for several decades, even Lasswell noted most of these research concerns focused upon senders, messages, receivers and effects, with minimal interest in the channels communication was being disseminated through.

Of course, in Lasswell's time there were not very many channels available for communication dissemination. Just prior to the mid-point of the last century, he listed "radio, press, film" as the only communication channels scholars were researching. All of that changed dramatically with the introduction and then the development of television, but the greatest technological impact upon communication message delivery - the "channel" in terms of Lasswell's paradigm - came with the arrival of the Internet. The Internet represents a paradigmatic shift in communications and public relations, creating the possibility of fully two-way communications between organizations and their publics.

Since the Internet provides fast, easy, and immediate access to so much information it is having a unique impact on the way public relations is practiced. By utilizing its unlimited potential, the Internet has grown into an extremely powerful communication medium which public relations professionals simply can not ignore. Estimates suggest the Internet is now used for a variety of communications and information sharing tasks by more than 275 million people in at least 175 countries. And research strongly suggests people all over the world rely considerably upon the Internet for gathering information. There should be absolutely no question the Internet has developed into a magic communication machine.

In this chapter we can see the impact the Internet and other new technologies are having on three major groups of people - the general public, journalists, and public relations professionals. It also examines the perceived credibility of the Internet, and looks at what impact the new technologies are having on relationships between public relations professionals and journalists. Results of a variety of research studies are used to examine technology's impact upon the general public and journalists, and a special web-based survey was developed to obtain information about technology's effect on those who practice public relations.

The new technologies have radically changed how all three of these groups of people communicate. In a groundbreaking research study published in 2000, IMT Strategies estimated the Internet's impact on global commerce at less than one percent of the value of all global trade, but said the Internet's impact on communication throughout the world has been "logarithmically large. "

In addition to quickly becoming the world's largest information source, the Internet has rapidly developed into an important medium for the distribution of public relations messages. New technologies have dramatically changed the way public relations works by providing new and more efficient ways in which communication messages can be produced, distributed, displayed, and stored.

As public relations scholars Pavlik and Dozier have written, "little is known with great certainty about the future of the information superhighway except that the pace of technological change is likely to continue to accelerate. "Cutlip, Center, and Broom point out successful public relations professionals have been matching appropriate media with suitable messages since public relations began. They also say, "The Internet represents the most ubiquitous leading edge of what is a major communication revolution. The digital world has changed communication within organizations and between organizations and their various publics. "

Newsom, VanSlyke Turk, and Kruckeberg now say, "It is virtually impossible to effectively practice public relations today without using the Internet. "And, Wilcox, Ault, and Agee suggest, cyberspace communication is "a significant, swiftly expanding tool for public relations practitioners. "One Internet scholar says public relations professionals, journalists, and advertisers use the new technologies to work more effectively, and in the process work faster, more efficiently, and reduce costs in the process.

In 1998, Bunz found the Internet was having a strong impact on public relations in her survey of professionals in the US and seven other countries. Among other findings, Bunz reported boundary spanning activities such as two-way communication were being improved and facilitated through functions such as e-mail and the Internet. In addition to the obvious impact of providing organizations with an exciting communication medium offering unlimited message dissemination potential, the Internet also has provided that same opportunity for those wishing to distribute negative public relations messages. This has resulted in making the task of monitoring everything said about an organization on the Internet by friend and foe, an important component of contemporary public relations practice.

As Cutlip, Center, and Broom point out, "Rumors on the Internet have the potential to influence labor negotiations, attract regulatory attention, drive stock prices up or down, and increase or decrease sales. "Organizational reputations can be damaged, the value of brands can suffer, and goodwill can be diminished by those accessing the kind of uncontrolled and uncensored messages which have appeared on the Internet. Some refer to this as the Internet's "dark side" where the dissemination of false and misleading information can result in serious injury.

Jackson and Stoakes have urged public relations professionals to monitor cyberspace because, "rumors that originate on the Internet often make their way into print and broadcast media before a company ever knows they exist. "Two years ago, Ryan surveyed PRSA members and found 99 percent of them used computers to access the Internet. Duke surveyed science public relations practitioners and says they consider the Internet and e-mail essential in their work. She also reports Internet and e-mail use by journalists has increased media coverage of some organizations, because it is now easier for reporters to obtain information.

Some claim the most effective public relations use of the Internet has been made by special interest groups such as environmentalists and hundreds of nongovernmental organizations (NGOs) that have effectively used the new technologies to advance their positions and by doing so have gained ground with the media, government, and public opinion. Research has found many of these groups are successful because they have effectively used their web sites to build relationships with various publics. An equal amount of success has been accomplished via Internet web sites falling within the category which has become known as ACOs, an acronym for anti-corporate organizations and anti-capitalism organizations.

A variety of religious groups also have used the Internet with considerable effectiveness,There is even a recently revised and updated book - full of practical information written in an easy-to-understand format -

designed to help Christians make effective use of the Internet. Most websites hosted by corporations and public relations agencies concentrate upon information dissemination or communication outputs, but many special interest, NGO, and ACO web sites focus on communication outcomes, and provide more interactive opportunities which enhance relationship development.

During the early years of the Internet's development many communication scholars did not view it as a mass medium. The attitude expressed by DeFleur and Ball-Rokeach in 1989 was typical of many leaders in the communication field. They dismissed the idea of the Internet being a form of mass communication, and compared computers to telephones saying, "Even if computer literacy were to become universal, and even if every household had a personal computer equipped with a modem, it is difficult to see how a new system of mass communication could develop from this base alone. "

Rankow says similar apprehensions about communication potential were apparent shortly after development of the telephone as a means of communication. Fortunately, communication scholars have come to accept the Internet as the powerful information medium it is. Middleberg believes public relations professionals are making effective use of the Internet.

However, IMT Strategies, which recently surveyed 100 US public relations professionals in an attempt to define what kinds of impact the Internet was having on the field, say public relations people have not yet come to understand the impact the Internet could have on their field. Results of this survey found the new technologies have provided public relations professionals with the ability to communicate with more targeted audiences and more media, but suggest these new technologies have not yet been used to their full potential. And, the Internet also has provided a medium which makes it possible to bypass other media and permit communication directly from an organization to its customers, stockholders, employees, and other strategic publics.

The global Internet which has played such a major role in the development of communication and public relations had its roots as a Cold War project nearly half a century ago, and originally was designed for US military communication in the event of a Soviet Union nuclear strike. The birth of computer versions of the Internet can be traced to 1957 when the USSR launched Sputnikl I, a earth orbiting satellite prompting the US to create the Advanced Research Projects Agency (ARPA) within the Ministry of Defense. In addition to being the technological think-tank of American defense efforts, ARPA opened a computer research program in 1962.

In 1969 additional developments took place with electronic connections of researchers who were working on a Department of Defense project at four US universities. ARPA's network grew throughout the 1970s, and the first e-mail program was introduced by Ray Tomlinson in 1972. The restrictive nature of ARPA led to the development of several additional networks such as Usenet, BITNET, and Fidonet which provided greater public access to technologies being used on the APRANET. The concept of Domain Name Servers (DNS) was introduced in 1984. This initiated the development of categories into US Internet addresses - such as ". com" (commercial), ". org" (international organizations), ". edu" (educational institutions), and ". gov" (government agencies) -along with a series of codes for other countries.

The Internet continued to develop when a number of national governments encouraged its use through higher educational systems. In the US, for example, the Internet is one of the few technologies that developed more fully within universities and higher education than within public and private organizations. The concept of the World Wide Web was enhanced in 1989 when British researcher Tim Berners-Lee created HTML, thus permitting the transmission of text, pictures, and sound in a single format. According to Griffi:hs,in 1994 there were about three million domain hosts and approximately 3,000 web sites, and those numbers virtually have more than doubled each year since. At last count, late in 2000, there were 93 Million domain hosts and 10 Million web sites. The future of the Internet bids fair to be bigger and exponentially faster.

The degree of credibility audiences give the Internet when compared to other information media is a very important question for public relations because people are less likely to pay attention to media they do not perceive as credible. Studies on the credibility of newspapers, magazines, radio, and television continually report if people do not believe what they read, see, and hear, they are less likely to pay attention to it. And, as Johnson and Kaye point out," lack of trust in information obtained from the Web could keep it from becoming a major source of news. "The belief some information sources are more reliable than others dates back to ancient Greece and the work of Plato, Socrates, and Aristotle. Self recently reviewed these works and says sources have credibility if (a) "their message's rightness is perceived by the audience," (b) "they rightly read how to reveal themselves to particular audiences," and © "because of audience characteristics. "

Severin and Tankerd suggest credibility research in communication is closely connected to research in the areas of persuasion and attitude change. Even though Internet and web-based information is potentially inaccurate and biased, research is finding people increasingly rely upon it as an information medium. Callahan claims journalists make considerable use of Internet as an information gathering tool. And, a 1999 study found 97 percent of American journalists have used the Internet indirectly in researching information for news stories, while 73 percent have used it directly. Although most studies appear to find Internet information to be about as credible as that received from traditional news sources, some report web-based information as being the most credible.

Some studies have found no significant differences between the credibility of Internet information and that obtained from more traditional media sources. Other research reports Americans find Internet information to be as credible as that obtained from television, radio, and magazines, but not as credible as newspaper information. A significant variable in the perception of Internet credibility is the fact information can be placed online without editorial filters so prevalent with the other mass media such as newspapers, magazines, radio, and television.

Starobin points out traditional news sources are subject to a variety of social and professional pressures which require accurate and unbiased dissemination of information, but says the Internet is not subject to similar constraints. Johnson and Kaye agree. Since the Internet does not utilize the same gatekeeping functions as traditional news media, White believes some organizations now bypass the news media and manage communication directly between the company and specific target audiences.

Flannigan and Metzger say some information obtained via the Internet might be "dubious or difficult to appraise. " The Internet might level the playing field between large and small organizations, since it provides easy opportunities for those opposed to a company to come together in communication. This unique characteristic of the Internet is fostering new concerns about the honesty and integrity of information distributed via the Internet. The most important component in credibility and believability of information contained on the Internet is the source of the information.

Some web sites are considered more credible than others, and some sources are more believable than others. Sundar found direct quotes from reliable sources enhanced the perceived credibility of online news stories. Although it was originally thought the factor structures relating to perceived credibility might be different for printed and online information, recent research finds a striking similarity between the two. This suggests the same rules apply when comparing the perceived credibility of online and printed information.

Another important concern regarding credibility and believability of Internet messages for public relations professionals relates to how reliable journalists consider information delivered to them via cyberspace. The leading problems journalists have in using online sources are

(a) verification of facts,

(b) web sites containing unreliable information,

(c) badly sourced information, and

(d) lack of source credibility.

Essentially then, all factors being equal, information delivered via the Internet has the potential to be perceived as being just as credible and believable as information delivered through any other mass communication source, provided the Internet information originated with a credible and believable source.

Impacts of Internet

Most public relations campaigns not only involve sending information to target audiences, but also require forming relationships with the receivers of these communication messages. In recent years a number of articles have appeared on topics concerning technical, legal, ethical, and other issues involving the public relations and the Internet. However, there is a scarcity of research on how the new technologies are impacting relationships between public relations professionals and journalists.

Although not specifically addressing relationships, Duke reports the public relations professionals she surveyed make considerable use of e-mail but do not believe it ever will replace face-to-face communication as the best way to interact with journalists. Hon and Grunig call building relationships with key publics the fundamental goal of public relations. They stress, "Public relations practitioners need special skills to negotiate relationships with management and with multiple publics because maintaining relationships with one public may make it difficult to maintain a relationship with another public with competing goals. "Cutlip, Center, and Broom insist the relationships between senders and receivers of public relations messages deliver a huge impact on the communication process.

In the early development of public relations, research designed to evaluate effectiveness almost always focused upon communication outputs. Such measures concentrated on messages themselves and the amount of attention or exposure a public relations effort received. Later, evaluation research would focus upon communication outcomes measuring whether or not messages actually reached their intended audiences, and whether or not the messages were understood, were paid attention to, and were retained. These studies also looked for any evidence suggesting the messages resulted in any change in opinion, attitude, or behavior.

Output and outcome measurements both focus upon short-term successes and the real value of a sustained public relations campaign can only be evaluated by examining the impact of long-term relationships developed between an organization and its publics. Today, most public relations scholars believe the best way to determine the value of public relations is by measuring the quality of relationships an organization has with its strategic publics. Most business leaders agree.

Information is power and it's all there on the web. Business is still about relationships, and technology can help us build and maintain those relationships. And, some are now encouraging communication researchers to become more active investigating how the new technologies are changing the roles and jobs of professional communicators. The realities of postmodern life are changing the way people view themselves and their relationships, and suggests the Internet, global jet-lag, and the influence of modern media coverage, are all impacting the way people now think about themselves and the people around them.

Internet has dramatically changed many relationships because so many people now transmit information to individuals they cannot see. Using several modern communication technologies - cell phones, e-mail, and the

Internet - to make the point, transmitting information is the secondary purpose of communication, and insists conservation and relationship development should be the primary purpose of communication.

Bertman believes the accelerated pace of technological and social change has eroded the essence of American society's fundamental values, and argues for a drastic slowdown which would permit people to reassert control over the technologies that now dominate their lives. Borgmann says the world abounds with information because the Internet and other technologies represent the most prominent layer of the current cultural landscape, and he calls for "... a theory and an ethics of information theory to illuminate the structure of information and an ethics to get the moral of its development. "

Some research about the Internet's impact upon relationships has appeared in social science literature, particularly in psychology. Donn, et al., suggest interpersonal relationships can be formed and fostered on the Internet. Suler not only calls cyberspace "the new frontier in social relationships," but also says Internet relationships might be better in some ways than interpersonal or face-to-face ones. Faloutsos reports cyberspace and the Internet are turning a lot of face-to-face and interpersonal relationships into virtual ones.

A few studies have started to surface measuring the potential impact of romantic relationships that are either formed and/or maintained through Internet communication. Essentially these articles suggest romantic relationships carried out over the Internet have both advantages and disadvantages.

The Internet audience continues to grow each year, and is becoming decidedly mainstream. One of the most thorough landmark research studies examining the impact of the Internet on people's everyday lives is the annual America Online/Roper Starch Cyberstudy which has been conducted each year since 1998. Using a random sample of more than one thousand Americans, this research provides compelling evidence indicating going online is becoming an important part in many people's lives. The rate of consumer purchasing online is showing phenomenal growth. Recent research results suggest the majority of Americans who use the Internet say they go online to make purchases.

The proportion of American Internet users who went online for commercial purposes nearly doubled between 1998 and 2000, and these increases were noted in all areas of commerce including making purchases, booking travel reservations/tickets, and even online banking. Americans also are spending more money online each year, with the average Internet user having approximately $500 in such expenditures every three months. The number of people who agree they will increase the amount of purchases they make in the future also has risen considerably. When the first research studies investigating online use were conducted six or seven years ago the majority of Internet users were well-educated, affluent men.

Increasingly, however, women, people with modest incomes, and those without university educations have joined the ranks of Internet users. One study found Americans with online connections in their homes during 2000 mirrored the nation's population to a greater extent than those who had home access previously. Another piece of research suggests the Interned is having an even greater impact among younger and bettereducated people, claiming more university graduates under 50 years of age go in the Internet each day than regularly watch a nightly network television broadcast.

The Pew Research Center has extensively studied how Americans use the new communication technologies and claims the Internet, "is clearly changing the way Americans live. "This research suggest the Internet is attracting key segments of the national audience, and also points out Americans appear to have a tendency to pay attention to national news only when something of great importance is happening. The America Online/Roper Starch Worldwide Adult 2000 Cyberstudy said this about the adult American online audience in 2000:

For the first time in 2000, more women (53%) than men (47%) went online in the US, and nearly as many women (49%) as men (51%) are now able to access the Internet from their homes. The 53% to 47% reflects the true gender proportions in the US' general population. After years of reporting most Americans who went online were university educated, results now suggest educational attainment of Internet users has shifted more in the direction of general public norms. Of the Americans who went online during 2000, one-third (33%) have a high school education or less, up from 22% in 1999.

The average income level of people who go online also is changing. In 2000, 24 percent of those who went online had household incomes of less than $35,000, up from 11 percent a year earlier. Research suggests the Internet has become a major news source which is attracting key segments of the national news audience. Although the Pew Research Center reports more Americans get their news from television than from the Internet, regular television news viewership has fallen in recent years while use of the Internet as a news source has increased. The only exception to this trend appears to revolve around coverage of major news events.

For example, during the first few days of the crisis following terrorist attacks on the United States on September 11, 2001, 78 percent of the American public reported they followed the news very closely. Most (92%) of those seeking news about these terrorist attacks listed television as their major source of news. Only three percent listed the Internet. And, television audiences that week were huge. Nielsen rating numbers suggest nearly 80 million people in 69 percent of the nation's television homes watched TV coverage on September 11. One reason for the lower than usual use of the Internet during a national crisis of this nature relates to the reality at exceptional times, when all television networks are providing live coverage of a news event, it frequently is faster for consumers to get news from television than from the Internet.

Chicago Tribune reporter James Coates also says many high-speed Internet functions were not technologically prepared to handle the millions of requests they received for access to web sites. This forced many news web sites to abandon color photographs, video, and other bells and whistles of high-bandwidth technology and convert into basic text messages on low-bandwidth levels that require only a small fraction of high-speed transmission capabilities. While a number of scholars and practitioners have conducted research designed to examine how the Internet has impacted print and broadcast journalism, two of the major pacesetters in this area of study are Don Middleberg and Steven Ross.

Middleberg, Chairman and CEO of Middleberg Euro RSCG, was one of the first public relations professionals to understand the impact the Internet would have on public relations. Ross, an associate professor at Columbia University's Graduate School of Journalism, is one of the nation's leading academic authorities on Internet and other new technologies used by journalists. Their research has chronicled journalists' use of the Internet through annual studies which began in 1995 and has explored the symbiotic relationship between the media and the Internet. Middleberg also has encouraged public relations professionals to combine traditional and digital media relations in their communication with journalists.

The most recent Middleberg and Ross survey, which included both print and broadcast journalists, found, "Reporters and editors' use of the Net for e-mail, article research, and finding story ideas, new sources and press releases is at an all-time high. " This 2001 report said 98 percent of the journalists surveyed check for e-mail messages daily, and spend an average of 15 hours per week sending and reading e-mail. Other findings include: Journalists believe the Internet has made their jobs easier and improved the quality of their work.

Most journalists enjoy using the Internet and predict reporters who avoid new technologies will not succeed in the future. The most popular uses of the Internet for journalists involve e-mail and article research. Many journalists say they use the Internet to add depth and breadth to news stories they write. The number of journalists who go online to conduct article research is increasing dramatically. In 2000, 81 percent of print journalists went online daily to conduct such research. In 1999 that figure was 73 percent. There has been a dramatic increase in Internet use for the development of news story ideas. More than eighty percent of print journalists search online daily. Company Web sites are gaining popularity as information sources especially when no other primary source is available.

More than two-thirds of American journalists now read publications online. One-third of all broadcast journalists want to download audio files from Web sites, and one-fifth want to receive video files. Journalists now rate e-mail equal to the telephone as the preferred medium for interviewing news sources. Seventy percent participate in dialogues with readers via e-mail or in discussion groups. Most journalists have at least two e-mail addresses. Fewer than ten percent of American journalists say they have no e-mail address. Although use of instant messaging by journalists' remains low, more become familiar with this technology each year. The 1999 study reported 76 percent never use instant messaging, but that figure was down to 56 percent in the 2000 study.

Each year more newspapers permit their Web sites to "scoop" their print product. Only 45 percent prevented this in 2000, down from 58 percent in 1999. Middleberg and Ross found 81 percent of US print journalists search online daily, but few use topic-specific search engines and many reporters lack knowledge about specialized Web sites. Only 44 percent said they would use Web chat or newsgroup postings as primary or secondary sources, and 47 percent said they would report or spread a story about information that started on the Web if it could be confirmed by an independent source. They also report e-mail and article research are the most popular online activities for journalists. In addition to the Middleberg and Ross study, research conducted by The Pew Research Center for The People and The Press, has found a rapid emergence of the Internet as a major news source. It also reported a significant decline in broadcast news viewership.

The Pew Research Center's report said, "Fully one-in-three Americans now go online for news at least once a week, compared to 20 percent in 1998. And 15 percent say they receive daily reports from the Internet, up from six percent two years ago. At the same time, regular viewership of network news has fallen from 38 percent to 30 percent over this period, while local news viewership has fallen from 64 percent to 56 percent. I t might be significant that the Internet is having such a huge impact as a highly requested information source during a time when cable television and satellite receivers have provided the American public with access to a seemingly unlimited number of television channels.

The Pew research indicates nearly 80 percent of all Americans have the capabilities to receive television broadcasts from either cable or satellites. Other findings of this research include: Americans who are interested in news and go online tend to watch less network television news. The new technologies appear to be having less of a direct negative impact on cable television news, radio and print media. It does not appear Internet use is causing people to spend less time than they normally did watching cable news channels, reading daily newspapers, or listening to radio news. All news outlets are being impacted by a slowly declining appetite for news by the American public. Less than half of the American public (45%) says it enjoys keeping up with the news a great deal.

Only 48% say they follow national news closely most of the time. Both of these percentages represent a slight decline from surveys conducted in earlier years This research found huge differences based upon age. Less than a third (31%) of young adults say they enjoy keeping up with the news. More than half (57%) of Americans age 50 and older enjoy following the news. Although younger Americans do not enjoy following news closely, they do appreciate the wide range of information sources available to them.

Older Americans who like following the news often feel overwhelmed by the increasingly crowed media landscape. Internet news is attracting both younger Americans with only a marginal interest in news, and older people. Internet news plays a larger role in the lives of those with access who do not enjoy the news than among those who do. Internet news with its headline news format and ability to deliver quick updates, is attractive to younger consumers.

At the same time, the Internet's ability to provide more depth on certain subjects also appeals to individuals with large news appetites, such as affluent college graduates. As many younger Americans turn to the Internet for news, the audience for traditional media is aging. The growth of Internet news has impacted the way Americans get business and financial information.

Among Americans who regularly trade stocks, the Internet has supplanted traditional media as the leading source for stock market quotes and investment advice. The ability of investors to customize their online stock portfolios definitely plays a factor in the popularity of Internet use for investment information. This revolution in financial news has had less of an impact on the general American public and on less than active investors. Still, 16% of all Americans said they would turn first to the Internet for news if the market were to drop 1,000 points.

The remote control is playing a major role in how Americans, especially young people, watch television news. Three-quarters of those under 20 say they watch television news with a remote control device in hand compared with 54 percent of those over 50. There are apparent gender differences in terms of Internet news interests between men and women. Technology is the top draw for men, with women most often seeking information about science and health.

Overall, the leading online news topic is weather. Additional research tells us newspapers also have lost ground to the Internet. In a large, national survey of media use, Stempel, Hargrove, and Bernt, found huge gains for Internet use for news and a decline for both local and network television news and for newspapers. Flanagin and Metzger found the Internet was used by information seekers more than books, magazines, newspapers, the telephone, electronic mail, or face-to-face communication. When comparing those who use the Internet for news and those who do not, this research found Internet users were more likely than non-users to be newspaper readers and radio news listeners.

The Internet has radically altered the nature of communications. This has important consequences for the way organizations share and distribute information with their customers, key constituencies and the general public. In the past, information flows were mostly linear and hierarchical, and easy for organizations to influence or control - e.g., via public relations and mass media advertising. The Internet will change this. The open, interconnected nature of the Internet is replacing this linear information "supply chain" with a network-based, peer-to-peer communication model that lacks clear locus points.

The impact that the Internet has had on global commerce can be measured as a tiny fraction: under 1% of the value of all global trade is yet done online. By contrast, the impact of the Internet on global communications has been logarithmically large: in the space of a decade the number of people communicating online went from thousands to hundreds of millions. IMT Strategies conducted in-depth interviews with more than 100 marketing and communications professionals at large traditional businesses, new Internet firms, offline and online media, public relations firms, marketing agencies and specialized communications consultancies. This research makes clear that public relations and communications specialists are struggling to recognize the impact that the Internet will have on how communication occurs. They are reacting slowly to the changes it will make in online business and culture.

The new mix of PR services will incorporate elements of management consulting, business intelligence, publishing, direct marketing and Internet strategy. Considering that U.S. businesses today spend nearly one-third of one trillion dollars annually on the above services, the public relations industry could double its U.S. 1999 annual billings ($3 billion) by siphoning off a mere 1% of the service fees spent on those industries with a new hybrid set of marketing communications skills.

Public relations and communications professionals must demonstrate mastery of these new communications models and leadership to their clients. To date, many communications agencies are not feeling immediate pain due to growth in demand for their services as a result of a strong economy and the (waning) demand boom of Internet businesses hungry for name recognition. This near-term growth is masking the need to rapidly evolve the role of communications services for long-term relevance.

Compounding this, communications services are not leveraging technology as well as other marketing disciplines and are generally thin on innovation. As communications become more networked and complex, client organizations will place more emphasis on communications strategy and

Howard, C.M. 1998. How your Employee Communications Programs Can Boost Productivity and Pride. *Public Relations Quarterly*. Fall 1998. 43(3): 15-23

Hunt, T. & Grunig, J.E. 1994. "Public Relations Techniques". Forth Worth: Harcourt Brace College Publishers.

White, C., Raman, N. 1999. "The World Wide Web as a Public Relations Medium: The Use of Research, Planning, and Evaluation in Site Development". *Public Relations Review*. Vol 25(4): 405-419 White, J; Mazur, L.1995.

Index

Abraham Maslow 168
Action-Image continuum 117
Anti-capitalism organizations 272
Anti-corporate organizations 272
Anti-drunk driving campaign 56
Apathy 15
Audience participation 202

China Construction Bank (CCB) 256, 264
Christianity 49
Collaborative publishing systems 182
Collectivism 253
Communications Audits 115
Community relations focus 108
Conservatism 65
Consumer organization 190
Cooperative willingness 62
Corporate philanthropy 108
Corporatization of media 171
Crystallizing Public Opinion, 3
Culture Variation 252

Democratization 186
Deontology 49
Domain Name Servers (DNS) 274

E-commerce 248
Ego-driven surface 169
Emotional appeal 54
Emotional energy 118
Employee volunteerism 108
Entertaining communications 174
Ethical performance 51
Ethical principles 110
Ethics Systems 49
European Union (EU) 3
External Interviews 116

Face-to-face communication 288
Free-lance technicians 70

Gut-wrenching reaction, 59

Hierarchical cultures 251
High-visibility business 107
Hostility 13
Human Resources (HR) 69

Individualism 253
Instant Messenger (IM) 200
Internal accounting system 183
International public relations 248
International repercussions 7
Internet community 210
Investment value 12
Irish Blood Transfusion Service (IBTS) 14

J. Grunig 249

Ledbetter Lee 1
Localization features 19

Market fluctuations 171
Media Campaign Kits 22
Media organizations 168, 191
Metabolism 63
Modern public relations 248
Modern-day public relations 1
Multiple Image 17

Non-priority issues, 112

One-way communication 250
Online information, 19
Online participation i 174
Online social forms 171
Open-source style guide 208
Organizational goals 66

Participatory journalism 176
Persuasive advocacy 112
Pew Internet & American Life Project, 170
Political maneuvers 171
Post media kit 20
Print Media 20
Professional organization 51
Psychic value 11
Public relations campaign 5
Public Relations Profession 47
Public Relations Tools 18
Public Service Announcements (PSAs) 55
Publicity 4

Radio Public Service Announcements 22
Reputation systems 178, 180
Reputational Tracking 53
Reputations systems 183

Scalable Virtual Staff 202
Scott Rosenberg 197
Shanghai Pudong Development Bank (SPDB) 259
Social recognition 169
Social responsibility 54
Societal Alignment 121
State-of-the-art technology 123
Stereotyped relationship 257
Strong management 112

Teleological ethicists 49
Teleology 49
Three Pillars of Societal Alignment 123
Time management skills 9
Transparency 110
Two-way communication 122
Two-way symmetrical model 121, 249

Values-Image Continuum 110
Virtual communities 168

Workplace environment 54
World Trade Organization (WTO) 262
World Wide Web (WWW) 68, 267